# The Corruption of the Curriculum

# The Corruption of the Curriculum

Shirley Lawes, Michele Ledda,
Chris McGovern, Simon Patterson,
David Perks, Alex Standish

Introduction by
Frank Furedi

Robert Whelan (Editor)

Civitas: Institute for the Study of Civil Society
London
Registered Charity No. 1085494

mT

First Published June 2007

ISBN (13) 978-1-903386-59-0

Independence: The Institute for the Study of Civil Society
(Civitas) is a registered educational charity (No. 1085494)
and a company limited by guarantee (No. 04023541). Civitas
is financed from a variety of private sources to avoid over-
reliance on any single or small group of donors.

All publications are independently refereed. All the Institute's
publications seek to further its objective of promoting the
advancement of learning. The views expressed are those of
the authors, not of the Institute.

Typeset by
Civitas

Printed in Great Britain by
The Cromwell Press
Trowbridge, Wiltshire

12/19/08

# Contents

# Authors

**Frank Furedi** is Professor of Sociology at the University of Kent in Canterbury. His research is oriented towards the study of the impact of precautionary culture and risk aversion on Western societies. In his books he has explored controversies and panics over issues such as health, children, food and cultural life. His writings express a concern with the prevailing regime of cultural confusion towards valuing intellectual and artistic pursuits and with the difficulty that society has in providing a challenging education for children and young people. His books include: *Politics of Fear: Beyond Left and Right* (2005); *Where Have All the Intellectuals Gone: Confronting 21st Century Philistinism* (2005); *Therapeutic Culture: Cultivating Vulnerability in an Anxious Age* (2004); *Culture of Fear* (2002); and *Paranoid Parenting* (2001); His new book *Invitation to Terror* is to be published in October 2007.

**Shirley Lawes** is currently Subject Leader for Modern Foreign Languages at the Institute of Education, University of London. Before moving into higher education, she worked for many years as a teacher of French in secondary schools, further and adult education and industry. Shirley is editor of the journal *Francophonie* and has published widely on modern languages teaching and learning, and initial teacher training.

**Michele Ledda** teaches English at secondary level and has also taught French and Latin. He has an Italian degree in English Language and Literature and holds an MA by research in English from Leeds University, with a dissertation on James Joyce's *Ulysses* and Petronius's *Satyricon*. He collaborates with the education section of the Manifesto Club (www.manifestoclub.com) which campaigns for an elitist education for all, and has written various articles on education both for academic journals and for online magazines.

**Chris McGovern** has 32 years of teaching experience, at all ages from 5 to 18 and in both the maintained and the independent sectors. He has been head of history in two large comprehensive schools and is currently headmaster of an independent preparatory school in North London. He is a qualified Ofsted and ISI inspector. In the 1980s he helped to found the History Curriculum Association and remains a director. During the 1990s he served on two government advisory bodies: the School Examinations and Assessment Council and the School Curriculum and Assessment Authority. As a member of the group that revised the National Curriculum for history in the mid-1990s he published a critical minority report. He has been an education adviser to the Policy Unit at 10 Downing Street under two prime ministers and a member of the TUC local government committee. He is a regular contributor to press, TV and radio discussion of educational matters at home and abroad.

**Simon Patterson** has 30 years of teaching experience at degree level, in philosophy and related subjects, but his critique of the national curriculum in mathematics is based on his exposure to it as a trainee teacher on the Graduate Teacher Programme in 2001/2. He came to feel that the syllabus he and his colleagues were attempting to teach sought to cover too many disparate topics and that the practice of returning to the same topic year after year, and the rigid constraints on time this imposed, tended to de-motivate students and contributed to a culture of under achievement.

**David Perks** is head of physics at Graveney School, London. After completing his PGCE at Oxford he went straight into teaching and now has 20 years of teaching experience in state schools. He campaigns for the teaching of science through separate academic disciplines and writes regularly on education issues, with a focus on defending academic science education in schools.

**Alex Standish** is Assistant Professor of Geography, Department of Social Studies, Western Connecticut State University. Dr Standish recently received a doctorate in geography from Rutgers University in New Jersey. His thesis looked at the changing relationship between geography education and citizenship in schools. Previously, he completed a master's degree in education at Canterbury Christ Church University College in the UK. He has also taught in both primary and secondary schools in the southeast of England. Alex Standish has emerged as one of the few critics of new directions in geography education. He has debated the future of geography at the Geographical Association's annual conference and on BBC radio's Today programme. He also writes for *spiked-online* and the *Times Educational Supplement.*

**Robert Whelan** is Deputy Director of Civitas. His books include *The Corrosion of Charity; Involuntary Action: How Voluntary is the 'Voluntary' Sector?; Helping the Poor: Friendly visiting, dole charities and dole queues;* and *Octavia Hill's Letters to Fellow-Workers 1871-1911* (ed.). He is a director of the New Model School Company, set up under the auspices of Civitas, which aims to bring independent schooling within the reach of more parents, and he teaches English to Bengali students at a Saturday school in Bethnal Green.

# Editor's Preface

The problem that faces the editor of a multi-author volume is that the chapters may not all fit together. Sometimes authors seem to be travelling in different directions, and give the impression that they should be appearing in separate books.

That has not been a problem with *The Corruption of the Curriculum*. Our contributors, all of whom write from practical experience in the classroom, identify certain problems that occur in all of the subject areas. Traditional academic subjects are being drained of their intellectual content in favour of promoting concerns about racism, the environment, gender and other topics. Classes must be judged by children to be interesting and relevant to their day-to-day lives. Politicians are interested in education as a means of increasing GDP, and thus raising more taxes, while the methods being applied are very unlikely to achieve even that non-educational goal. Teachers are no longer treated as professional people, capable of exercising judgment, but are micro-managed by Whitehall, where every hour of their day is prescribed.

In Shakespeare's *Henry VI Pt 2* the anarchist rebel Jack Cade makes grammatical knowledge a capital offence:

> It will be proved to thy face that thou hast men about thee that usually talk of a noun and a verb, and such abominable words as no Christian ear can endure to hear.   (IV, 7)

Many young people emerging from eleven years of compulsory state education would be in no danger from Jack Cade's insurgents, because they would be unable to distinguish between a noun and a verb. But every subject has its own grammar, its corpus of knowledge that a teacher passes on to students, without which a grasp of the subject must remain forever out of reach. It is out of concern for these traditional disciplines that the authors of this collection of essays have raised the standard of defiance against the Jack Cades of the educational establishment.

I would like to thank Claire Fox and her colleagues at the Institute of Ideas, without whom this book would not have happened. It is a lonely business, defending high culture and academic rigour, and you need to know who your friends are.

Robert Whelan

# Introduction:
# Politics, Politics, Politics!

# Frank Furedi

Over the past two decades the school curriculum has become estranged from the challenge of educating children. Pedagogic problems still influence official deliberations on the national curriculum, but issues that are integral to education have become subordinate to the imperative of social engineering and political expediency. As I write this essay I receive word that the Equal Opportunities Commission has just dispatched 40 pages of guidance to head teachers and governors in England about how they should go about tackling inequality between the sexes. The guideline, *The Gender Equality Duty*, is the product of an imagination that regards the curriculum as principally a political instrument for changing attitudes and behaviour. 'The gender equality duty presents a fantastic opportunity for schools to make a coordinated effort to tackle inequality and ensure that all pupils are able to fully achieve their potential' declares the Commission.[1] Instructions to schools about how to close the gender gap compete with directives that outline how children should be taught to become more sensitive to cultural differences. Everyone with a fashionable cause wants a piece of the curriculum. The former national chair of the Professional Association of Teachers wants pupils to 'learn about nappies' and has demanded the introduction of compulsory parenting classes for 14- to 16-year-olds.[2] Others insist that teachers spend more time talking to their class about sex or relationships or climate change or healthy eating or drugs or homophobia or Islamophobia.

The school curriculum has become a battleground for zealous campaigners and entrepreneurs keen to promote their message. Public health officials constantly demand more compulsory classroom discussions on healthy eating and obesity. Professionals obsessed with young people's sex lives insist that schools introduce yet more sex education initiatives. Others want schools to focus more on black history or gay history. In the recent widespread media outcry over the sordid scenes of moral and cultural illiteracy on *Celebrity Big Brother*, many demanded that schools should teach Britishness. The Government hasn't yet announced any plans for introducing Appropriate Behaviour on Reality TV Shows into the curriculum... but nevertheless, Alan Johnson, the current education secretary, is a very busy man. Not only is he introducing global warming studies, he has also made the instruction of Britain's involvement in the slave trade a compulsory part of the history curriculum.

For Johnson, the subject of history, like that of geography, must be subordinated to the task of transmitting the latest fashionable cause or value. Johnson is indifferent to the slave trade as part of an academic discipline with its own integrity; rather he sees slave trade studies as a vehicle for promoting his version of a multicultural Britain. 'This is about ensuring young people understand what it means to be British today',[3] he said in defence of his reorganisation of the history curriculum. Johnson's title, education secretary, is something of a misnomer. He seems to have no interest in education as such. His preoccupation is with using the classroom to transmit the latest and most fashionable prejudices. He can't even leave school sports alone, recently announcing that PE lessons will now stress the importance of a healthy lifestyle and will raise awareness about the problem of obesity. So after children have received instruction on how to behave as green consumers, learned crucial parenting skills and feel very British, they'll be taught how and why to lose weight. A curriculum devoted to a total makeover has little energy left for dealing with such secondary issues as how to gain children's interest in real education.

Increasingly the curriculum is regarded as a vehicle for promoting political objectives and for changing the values, attitudes and sensibilities of children. Many advocacy organisations who demand changes to the curriculum do not have the slightest interest in the subject they wish to influence. As far as they are concerned they are making a statement through gaining recognition for their cause in the curriculum. The Government too is in the business of statement-making. It may lack an effective drugs policy but at least it can claim that schools provide drugs education.

In recent months the politicisation of the curriculum has acquired a powerful momentum. Back in February climate change emerged as the new Big Theme for the curriculum. According to proposals published by the Department of Education, cautionary tales about global warming will become integral to the British school curriculum. This instruction about global warming will masquerade under the title 'geography lessons'. As Alex Standish argues in his essay 'Geography Used To Be About Maps', this subject has been transformed into a crusade for transmitting 'global values'. And global values usually mean the latest Hurrah Causes championed by the cultural elites through the media. This was the intention behind Alan Johnson's announcement in February 2007 that: 'we need the next generation to think about their impact on the environment in a different way'. This project, aimed at manipulating how children lead their lives, is justified through appealing to a higher truth. Johnson claims that: 'if we can instil in the next generation an understanding of how our actions can mitigate or cause global warming, then we lock in a culture change that could, quite literally, save the world'.[4] Literally save the world!

That looks like a price worth paying for fiddling with the geography curriculum.

This ceaseless attempt to instil in schoolchildren fashionable values is symptomatic of a general state of moral confusion today. Instead of attempting to develop an understanding of what it means to be a good citizen, or articulate a vision of public good, Britain's cultural elites prefer to turn every one of their concerns into a school subject. In the classroom, the unresolved issues of public life can be transformed into simplistic teaching tools. Citizenship education is the clearest example of this corruption of the curriculum by adult prejudices. Time and again, school inspectors have criticised the teaching of citizenship, which is not really surprising considering that leading supporters of citizenship education seem to have little idea what the subject is or ought to be about.

Nick Tate, former chief executive of the Qualifications and Curriculum Authority, argued that citizenship education was 'about promoting and transmitting values', 'participation' and 'duties'. But the obvious question, 'values about what?', was carefully avoided. Instead, those advocating citizenship education have cobbled together a list of unobjectionable and bland sentiments that have been rebranded as values. Alongside fairness, honesty and community, even participation and voting have been turned into values.

A few years down the road and the meaning of citizenship is even less clear than when schools started teaching it as a subject. Back in January 2007, a review of how schools teach citizenship found that the subject failed to communicate any sense of what it means to be British. Anyone with the slightest grasp of pedagogy will not be surprised by the failure of successive social engineering projects in the classroom. The absence of any moral consensus in Britain today will not be solved through subjecting children to sanctimonious platitudes. Those who are genuinely interested in educating children and inspiring them to become responsible citizens will instead look to real subjects, which represent a genuine body of knowledge. Propaganda campaigns around the latest fashionable 'value' only distract children from learning. Values-led education has helped create a situation where children learn that the Holocaust was awful, but do not know which country suffered the greatest number of casualties during the Second World War. It will produce children who know that the slave trade was bad, but who are ignorant about how the right to vote was won in Britain.

The essays by Michele Ledda, Alex Standish, Chris McGovern, Shirley Lawes, Simon Patterson and David Perks in this collection deal with different school subjects. But they all point to similar problems that afflict their area of specialty. Their accusation about the corruption of the school curriculum is not made in the spirit of polemical excess. Corruption in these cases refers to the erosion of the integrity of education through debasing and altering its meaning. As a result some subjects such as geography and history no longer bear any resemblance to what they were in the past. At least the new dumbed-down happy versions of science and mathematics bear some relation to their subjects. But history without chronology is like learning maths through skipping over the multiplication table.

## The uniqueness of twenty-first century philistinism

Of course there is nothing new about attempts to influence the values and beliefs transmitted through the school curriculum. Competing claims made on the curriculum reflect confusion and an absence of consensus about how to socialise children. At least in part, the 'crisis of education' is symptomatic of an absence of consensus about the basic values of society. Back in the early 1960s the social philosopher Hannah Arendt recognised the tendency to confuse the lack of moral consensus in society with the problem of schooling. There had to be a measure of consensus about the past before a system of education could affirm its virtues. 'The problem of education in the modern world lies in the fact that by its very nature it cannot forego either authority or tradition, and yet must proceed in a world that is neither structured by authority nor held together by tradition' she wrote in 1961.[5] In other words, the crisis in education is often a symptom of a more fundamental erosion of authority and tradition. The diminishing relevance of the values of the past is a constant theme that underpins debates about education.

Arendt was one of the few observers to note that in a changing world society finds it difficult to establish a creative balance between the achievements and legacy of the past and the provision of answers to new questions and challenges thrown up in the present. It is because it is so difficult to mediate between old and new that educators continually experience their profession as facing a crisis. The challenge of sustaining respect for the past and being open to change can provide important insights about how to go about the business of teaching and learning and developing new knowledge. Unfortunately in recent decades the British education establishment has become estranged from this challenge. It has distanced itself from the past and devotes itself to searching for and inventing values 'appropriate' for our times. Indeed, one of its distinct characteristics is its obsessive search for novelty.

There is nothing unique about the experience of an education system in crisis. What is distinct about our time is the reluctance of educators to attempt to develop a system of schooling that can mediate between the old and the new. The growing tendency to reinvent subjects, modernise them or make them more relevant is driven by the objective of inventing a new tradition. Unfortunately traditions cannot be cobbled together out of thin air. If they lack an organic relationship to people's lived experiences they will lack a capacity to inspire. That is why every initiative taken to improve citizenship education falters and creates a demand for a new idea!

However, it would be wrong to perceive today's crisis of education as simply the contemporary version of an old problem. For a start education has become far more politicised than at any time during the past two centuries. When Blair made his famous 'education, education, education' speech what he really meant was 'politics, politics, politics'. In the absence of a consensus of what it means to be British and what are the fundamental values that society wishes to convey to young people, the curriculum has become subject to constant partisan disputes and political experimentation.

The contemporary crisis of education is subject to three destructive influences that are in many ways unique to our time. Firstly contemporary pedagogy has lost faith in the importance of knowledge and the search for the truth. Increasingly educators insist that there is no such thing as the truth and children are instructed that often there are no right or wrong answers. The relativistic turn in pedagogy has important consequences for epistemology and the quality of intellectual life in the west.[6] It also has profound implications for the way that the curriculum is perceived. If the meaning of the truth and the status of knowledge are negotiable, then so is the curriculum. Studying a subject or body of knowledge is rarely perceived as a good thing in itself. More importantly, the diminished status assigned to knowledge has encouraged a relativistic orientation towards standards. That is why officials have been so pragmatic about the way they wheel and deal about the content of school subjects. From their perspective, lowering standards has become the default position when confronted with a problem. Of course they rarely promote new initiatives through acknowledging that they have made the curriculum easier. Instead they suggest that the changes introduced make the subject more relevant and appropriate for our times. The recent announcement that delivery of education will become more personalised represents the logical outcome of this trend. Personalised learning displaces the idea that there is a coherent body of knowledge that needs to be assimilated in favour of the principle of teaching what works for the individual. Such a promiscuous attitude towards knowledge creates a situation where there are no real pedagogic barriers against pressures to politicise the curriculum.

The second destructive trend haunting education is the enthronement of philistinism in pedagogy. The striving for standards of excellence is frequently condemned as elitist by apparently enlightened educators. Forms of education that really challenge children and which some find difficult are denounced for not being inclusive. There have always been philistine influences in education but it is only in recent times that anti-intellectual ideals are self-consciously promoted by educators. The corrosive effects of anti-elitist sentiments are evident in all the subjects discussed by authors in this book.

The third important influence that is distinct to our times is a radically new way that children are perceived by educators. In recent decades it has become common to regard children as fragile, emotionally vulnerable things who cannot be expected to cope with real intellectual challenge. It was in this vein that in April 2007 teachers were instructed by Alan Johnson that they should routinely praise their pupils. According to guidelines, teachers ought to reward children five times as often as they punish them for disrupting lessons.[7] That this inane formulation of the relationship between praise and punishment is circulated through the institution of education is a testimony to the impoverished intellectual and moral climate that prevails in this domain. But the exhortation to institutionalise the praising of children is not an isolated attempt to flatter the egos of young people. Increasingly the therapeutic objective of making children feel good about themselves is seen as the primary objective of schooling.

The consequences of this tendency to infantalise children have been enormously destructive. At a time when Britain's schools face serious difficulties in providing children with a good education, they are to be charged with providing happiness lessons. This initiative is the latest technique adopted in a futile attempt to tackle the crisis facing the classroom through the management of children's emotions. Making children feel good about themselves has been one of main objectives of US schools during the past three decades. By the time they are seven or eight years of age, American children have internalised the prevailing psychobabble and can proclaim the importance of avoiding negative emotions and of high self-esteem. Yet this has had no perceptible impact on their school performance.

In Britain, too, educators who have drawn the conclusion that it is easier to help children feel good than to teach them maths, reading and science, have embraced the cause of emotional education. During the past decades they have also adopted a variety of gimmicks to improve classroom behaviour through helping children to relax. Some schools have opted for yoga, others use aromatherapy or chill-out music to improve concentration and learning. Perversely, the more we try to make children feel good about themselves, the more we distract them from engaging in experiences that have the potential for giving them a sense of achievement. These programmes encourage a mood of emotionalism in the school. I can predict with the utmost certainty that an expansion of the resources that schools devote to managing the emotional life of children will encourage pupils to turn inward and become even more preoccupied with themselves. Emotional education will have the unintended consequence of encouraging children to feel that they have a mental health problem. The branding of this therapeutic project as emotional education attempts to convey the impression that new forms of behaviour management possess educational value. They don't.

There are no easy magical solutions to the problems facing education. In one sense the system of education in a modern society will always be subject to new problems and challenges, but there are a number of steps that can be taken to restore a curriculum fit for our children. Firstly education needs to become depoliticised: politicians need to be discouraged from regarding the curriculum as their platform for making statements. Secondly society needs to challenge the tendency to downsize the status of knowledge and of standards. Anti-elitist education is in reality a masquerade for social engineering and needs to be exposed for its destructive consequence on school standards. Thirdly we need to take children more seriously, uphold their capacity to engage with knowledge and provide them with a challenging educational environment. They do not need to be made to feel good nor praised but taken seriously.

# English As A Dialect

## Michele Ledda

*English and national identity*

English is the subject that more than any other—perhaps even more than history—is bound up with national identity. That is why the uncertainty over what to teach in English to the young generation is as deep and widespread as today's uncertainty over what constitutes British values. But this is only one of the problems for English.

Another problem is that, with all the other traditional subjects, it is also one of the forms in which knowledge is organised, and just like any other subject that requires time, effort and discipline, English is accused of being elitist by educationalists who think that the majority of pupils are incapable of serious study or of much intellectual development.

The third problem is that, even if we thought children were capable of understanding difficult literary works and of learning the rules of their own language, we are not sure that this is desirable. Today we as a society have a very uneasy relationship with the past achievements of humanity, and often see human history as a litany of disasters rather than progress. The knowledge accumulated in the academic disciplines is therefore seen with suspicion, as part of the hubristic legacy of the Enlightenment, which has led to imperialism, modern warfare and environmental degradation, among other things. A fourth obstacle to the teaching of academic subjects is the idea that there is nothing more important than happiness or personal well-being. Intellectual development, important as this is, does not necessarily lead to happiness and it very often involves hard work, frustration, confusion and even boredom. Today it is

11

hard to justify teaching anything that is not enjoyable and both school pupils and university students are increasingly encouraged to adopt the passive attitude of the consumer.

A fifth problem is that the discipline itself has changed and has abdicated responsibility for determining the literary canon. Today literary critics in and outside the universities do not search for meaning, do not even try to exercise aesthetic judgment, but only aspire to personal, clever readings. In this climate, it is very difficult to justify any content in the curriculum as 'the best that has been written in English', and indeed the curriculum does not at the moment specify compulsory authors, except for Shakespeare. Still, someone has to choose some authors on which to test pupils in the exams. This task is almost completely arbitrary and is achieved through a secretive process, carried out by the examination boards, that has little to do with choosing the best texts but is driven instead by an attempt to represent all sections of British society.

The changes to the English curriculum over the past 20 years have already transformed the subject almost beyond recognition and the future changes, judging by the numerous government papers and the seemingly unstoppable drive towards personalised learning, will consign the systematic study of language and literature once and for all to the dustbin of history.

I will not attempt to deal with all of these aspects, but will concentrate on the contradictions between the general aims of the curriculum and the traditional purpose of a liberal education, which was to transmit knowledge to the next generation. I will look in particular at the choice of poems in the Assessment and Qualifications Alliance (AQA) *Anthology*[1] to illustrate the problems with devising an anthology which refuses aesthetic judgment as its main criterion for choice and uses instead the 'equal opportunities' method.

I will then explain how the 1989 Cox Report, which laid the foundations for the first English curriculum, was already informed by a great ambivalence towards English literature and towards Standard English and was unable to choose the literary texts and the content for a coherent programme of studies in English language.

Finally, I will look at the apparent contradiction of the periodic backlashes that arbitrarily attempt to impose isolated parts of the traditional liberal education, such as the National Literacy Strategy or the recent adoption of phonics, onto a child-centred, personalised education system that is founded on the rejection of a common body of knowledge. I will argue that both the trend towards personalisation and the tendency to go 'back-to-basics' share an inability to engage with our past in a critical, meaningful way.

### An anti-educational curriculum

'The curriculum in schools today resembles a dilapidated house on the outskirts of Mumbai', writes Anthony Seldon, education writer and Master of Wellington College.[2] 'The whole thing feels patched up and incoherent,' adds Peter Wilby, education journalist and former editor of the *Independent on Sunday* and of the *New Statesman*.[3] Both are responding to John White's pamphlet 'What schools are for and why'.[4]

The main argument in John White's latest work on the curriculum is that school subjects are too academic and outdated, 'a middle-class creation' that favours middle-class children, and that they should take an increasingly sub-sidiary role in favour of cross-curricular aims to do mainly with the child's well-being (echoing in this 'Every Child Matters') and encouraging children to adopt particular attitudes to 'liberal democratic values' and to the environment.

White, Seldon and Wilby are right in denouncing the incoherence of the present curriculum, torn as it is between the traditional aim of transmitting knowledge in the form of coherent disciplines and the new, ever-expanding aim of creating responsible, tolerant, happy, healthy, flexible, confident and successful citizens.

However, their solution would be to decrease the content that remains and make school subjects even more subservient to 'coherent' cross-curricular aims i.e. not ends in themselves but instruments in the formation of particular habits, attitudes and behaviour in the next generation. Only that which serves these aims should be taught in each subject.

The Qualifications and Curriculum Authority (QCA) also agrees that the National Curriculum should be modernised along the same lines. Its draft Programmes of Study for English at Key Stages 3 and 4 states first of all the justification for the existence of English in the Curriculum:

> Learning and undertaking activities in English contribute to achievement of the curriculum aims for all young people to become:
>
> - successful learners who enjoy learning, make progress and achieve
>
> - confident individuals who are able to live safe, healthy and fulfilling lives
>
> - responsible citizens who make a positive contribution to society.[5]

What is missing here is the most important aim of all: to produce educated citizens, which means, as far as English is concerned, intellectually autonomous adults with a good knowledge of English language and literature, which includes their historical development.

The education system should first and foremost promote the intellectual development of children through the transmission of knowledge, and academic disciplines and school subjects are the best and most coherent organisation of knowledge at present. While we should not *a priori* discount the possibility of a new and better way of organising knowledge, any changes to the curriculum should be made with the main goal of education in mind. However, the aims proposed by the QCA are worse than irrelevant. They are anti-educational.

Take the first aim. The aim of education should be to produce educated people, not successful learners. At the end of their secondary schooling, young adults should have learnt *something* about the world we live in. Above all, they should know about its past, about the history of humanity and our achievements in the various fields. As I will explain in greater detail with regard to English, this curriculum has been anti-educational from the start (1989) in that it has always sought to distance itself from the past achievements of humanity, from the knowledge accumulated in the various subjects.

The reason why children should be taught above all about the past, including the recent past, is that they will learn a great deal about the immediate present simply by growing up in today's society. But the world in which we live is also the product of events that have occurred in the past. Without knowing that, it is difficult fully to understand the present. As for learning about the future, that is the domain of astrologers and soothsayers.

Yet the current curriculum is based on the assumption that knowledge of the past is largely irrelevant to life in the modern world. It is shaped by an anxiety about the future, and about equipping children with the skills and attitudes that will help them lead a successful life in the modern world.[6] This anxiety derives in part from the fact that we seem to have lost a sense of direction and of identity, and feel uncertain about the path we should follow.

No one can predict the future and know in advance which particular skills will be of practical use in order to adapt to the future needs of society and the economy. That is why the Qualifications and Curriculum Authority doesn't quite know *what* children should learn, but it can state with confidence that the aim of the curriculum is to produce 'successful learners, who ... make progress and achieve'. To the fundamental question 'Successful at what?' or 'Achieve what?' the QCA has no answer. The aim is not any more to learn something but to learn how to learn, to become, not educated citizens but 'lifelong learners', in order to adapt to an unknown future.

The condition of the 'lifelong learner' is a condition of lifelong dependence[7] similar to the nightmare scenarios of Franz Kafka's and Robert Walser's expressionist novels, in which the protagonist is involved in a doomed struggle to achieve independence in an irrational, unknowable world ruled by arbitrary powers.

This condition of limited sovereignty is confirmed by the third aim on the QCA list, which also betrays the abandonment of liberal education and of democratic values, as the phrase 'responsible citizens' implies that citizens must display a behaviour that is deemed 'responsible' by the authorities. This is incompatible with the democratic ideal of the free citizen who makes autonomous decisions. Only children or subjects can be asked to behave responsibly. In the democratic ideal, free citizens are responsible by definition, as they have a sovereign, inalienable right to determine their country's policies through the democratic process and to reap the benefits or suffer the consequences of their choices.

### The literary canon is replaced by the equal opportunities form

'Of all traditional subjects,' according to John White, 'English, geography and science are perhaps the most adaptable [to the new instrumentalist ethos].'

And the English curriculum has indeed been changed beyond recognition, from the academic subject it once was, into an unsystematic, if not altogether incoherent, range of activities for the development of isolated skills.

I don't want to suggest that the English curriculum should never change. In fact, it has always changed, just like the literary canon. But the criterion for change, both in the curriculum and in the canon, was supposed to be the literary quality of the works to be studied. Now critics and academics believe neither in the possibility nor in the desirability of aesthetic judgment.

Yet, while we have a national system of examinations, or until we find a way of letting children choose what they want to study in English (an idea that would appeal to many contemporary educationalists and policy-makers), someone has to decide what texts our children will study and be tested on. Today's canon is mainly determined by behind-the-scenes decisions made by examination boards through complicated consultation processes which have very little to do with the quality of the works to be studied and more with a preoccupation to include every possible religion, ethnicity, or culture and to make sure that there is a gender balance.[8]

A typical example is the *AQA Anthology* for the GCSE courses in English and English Literature, and the way its poems are chosen. Anthology, according to the Greek etymology, means 'a collection of flowers'. It is supposed to be a collection of the best texts available. But if one looks at the choices made by AQA it is immediately clear that it reads like an equal opportunities form.

The part of the *Anthology* devoted to poetry is divided into two sections. Section 1 is made up of 16 'Poems from different cultures,' to be studied for the GCSE English examination. They are all contemporary poems from India (4), Pakistan (1), the Caribbean (5), Africa (3), Scotland (1), and the US (2). Nine of these poems are by men and seven by women. (Students usually study eight of them at most, as that is the number they need to know to answer the examination question, and they represent 7.5 per cent of the total GCSE mark in English and English Literature.)

Section 2 is made up of 48 poems to be studied for the English Literature examination. Thirty-two of them are poems from four contemporary British poets, two men and two women, with eight poems each. Candidates can choose to study only two of these four poets (16 out of 32 poems), but they can't be two men, or two women: they have to be one man and one woman.[9]

The remaining 16 poems form a group called Pre-1914 Poetry Bank and are arranged in no discernible order, other than a loose association by theme. It seems that a conscious decision has been made to avoid the most obvious chronological order. The past is treated ahistorically as a succession of different fashions where poets from previous generations have little influence on the next. It is just another country on the equal opportunities form so that all the boxes can be ticked and all the categories are included in this non-judgmental syllabus. The whole tradition of English poetry from its origins to 1914 is represented by 16 poems while modern poetry has three times as many, all of them written after the 1950s.

A British pupil can go through the school system and get the top marks in English and English Literature without knowing that Spenser, Milton or Pope ever existed, but having studied Carol Ann Duffy twice, both at GCSE and A-level. With all due respect to Carol Ann Duffy, she is on the syllabus, not because she is a greater poet than Milton, but because she is more 'relevant,' dealing as she does with very contemporary issues such as disaffected learners.

As she has her psychopathic young man say, 'Shake-speare ... was in another language' (Education for Leisure).

18

And so is John Milton, whereas Duffy's poems—just as much as those of Simon Armitage ('I have lived with thieves in Manchester')—are seen as closer to the interests of our disaffected youth, who for their part may beg to differ.

## An anti-educational curriculum from the start

From its inception in 1989, the English Curriculum has been an incoherent, contradictory document that does everything but what a curriculum is supposed to do: specify what schoolchildren should study. It is clear from the account that Brian Cox himself gives of the workings of his National Curriculum English Working Group that the main concern at the time was not so much to propose a good English curriculum, as to devise a curriculum that would not upset anyone, even at the cost of including statements that not only were contradictory towards one another, but also attacked the transmission of knowledge and undermined the very existence of a national curriculum.

The contradictory nature of the first English curriculum becomes clear in Cox's discussion of the concept of tradition. In the sub-chapter entitled 'An English Tradition?' Cox writes:

> The desire for a national culture is seen as damagingly conservative, often 'racist' and almost inevitably unsympathetic to the rights of women ... [cultural critic] Robert Scholes argues that conservatives desire a common curriculum—any common curriculum—because this would have a unifying effect upon a society that suffers from an excess of pluralism, and this unifying effect, an achieved cultural consensus, would in itself be a good thing for the country socially and politically. In England the desire for an 'English' tradition is said to hide a deep fear of our present multi-cultural society.[10]

Scholes's view has, of course, grave implications for the very existence of a national curriculum, yet Cox does not comment on it. He accepts it in a non-judgmental way, together with the opposite view that children should learn Standard English and study the 'racist' traditional literature.

Cox tries to strike a balance, to be unbiased, but in doing so he deprives his English curriculum of any vision. Worse still, he accepts the value of inclusiveness, which forbids one to judge. Such a value makes a mockery of all the values included, the condition for inclusion being that no one particular point of view is taken entirely seriously. The value of inclusiveness also makes it impossible to devise a coherent programme of studies, as any choice, any positive statement, would exclude another.

The idea that every view is equally valid reminds one of Irwin, the cynical teacher in Alan Bennett's play *The History Boys*, who sees truth as an irrelevance and education as the capacity to pass examinations, even at the cost of intellectual dishonesty.[11]

The National Curriculum English Working Group found it impossible to judge and therefore avoided responsibility for selecting texts, as 'the number of suitable authors would make any list quite impracticable'.[12] This is a breathtaking statement from a group whose responsibility it was to decide what children should study in English. It is also a ridiculous excuse, since this 'quite impracticable' task is passed on to examination boards, schools and teachers. After all, someone must decide what texts children will study.

The Cox committee, however, felt much more confident in laying down some of the criteria for selection, such as 'syllabuses must consist of both male and female authors'. As we have seen above, these external criteria, which have more to do with biology than with literature, are the main criteria followed by examination boards such as AQA in selecting the poems for the GCSE examination. Any arbitrary choice of texts will do for an education establishment that doesn't know how to make a case for the study of the best literary works.

Cox qualifies almost every statement in support of the teaching of English language and literature with a warning about the danger of propagating nasty stereotypes of an elitist, racist or sexist kind. Instead of transmitting enthusiasm about the subject, the first curriculum treats English as a powerful weapon of cultural imperialism, class domination and gender inequality, one that should be handled with extreme care by all good teachers.

So, for example, Cox warns that after post-modern theory we can't afford to ignore the dangers of transmitting knowledge. That is why his 'group was anxious that all teachers should understand and think about the ideological assumptions implied by their approach to the teaching of English, for this is one way to overcome dogmatism'.[13]

Cox displays a similar approach to the teaching of Standard English. He recommended that children should be taught Standard English because they need it to be successful in life, but at the same time considered Standard English not the neutral norm but a 'social dialect'.

He even felt it necessary to explain what every student of English knows, that Standard English was originally a particular dialect spoken in the South of England and was then adopted as the norm, as if the historical origin of a common English language invalidated its present status and function.

In the Cox Report, working-class children are seen almost as separate races, as children from 'different cultures' with their own local identities, while middle-class children who speak Standard English at home are yet another race with their own identity. When teaching Standard English, teachers have a duty to respect the child's language.

Again, as we have seen for the choice of literary works, the Cox committee, though it states that 'all pupils ... must be able by the age of 16 to use spoken and written Standard English', refuses to devise a national curriculum: 'In some schools, most pupils use spoken Standard English as *their native dialect*; in others, most have to learn it as an additional language. Therefore it was not possible for my Working Group to prescribe a single policy which would suit all circumstances.'[14]

Cox felt more confident in prescribing that 'schools should teach [Standard English] in ways which do not denigrate the non-standard dialects spoken by many pupils' and that 'it should not be introduced at too early a stage; teaching pupils a new dialect [i.e. Standard English] may be confusing when they are learning many other aspects of language use'.[15]

Cox warns of many dangers: 'Teaching Standard English demands great sensitivity from the teacher. It is dangerous to tell a five-year-old boy or girl that his or her mother uses language incorrectly. Adolescents are going to be embarrassed and ashamed if a teacher suggests that their dialect, which is part of their identity, must be radically changed.'[16]

But he gives no indication of how these dangers can be avoided: 'How to teach spoken Standard English needs continual discussion among teachers. I would not want anyone to think that we had provided the final word.'[17]

When the foremost authority on the English curriculum displays such uncertainty as to what and how teachers of English should teach, warning of so many dangers but unable to put forward a coherent and unequivocal argument in favour of the discipline, the result can only be to spread anxiety and confusion, both among teachers and among pupils.

This attitude to the teaching of English has created a climate in which those teachers who are enthusiastic about their subject are seen as reckless fanatics, as dinosaurs who risk damaging the children in their care.[18]

If it is difficult at the best of times to transmit knowledge to a class of 30 children; it is well-nigh impossible to teach your subject when you are constantly reminded that you should not believe in it.

The idea that Standard English is almost a dialect among many has remained firmly ingrained in official thinking. For instance, among the essential skills listed in the latest QCA paper on the English curriculum, 'pupils should be able to vary vocabulary, structures and grammar to convey meaning *including speaking Standard English fluently*'.[19] One would have thought that teaching pupils to speak English meant *exclusively* Standard English. But then a note specifies that, even when teaching Standard English, 'it is helpful to bear in mind the most common non-standard usages for the UK, such as ... *they was* ... *have fell* ... *them books* ...'[20]

It is not very clear what the QCA means by 'bear in mind'. Presumably it is a worthy attempt to 'raise awareness' among teachers about the need to respect pupils' native dialect. Here again the QCA follows Cox who wrote that: 'dialect features are not errors [...] but are characteristics of a pupil's native language'.[21]

We can only teach effectively if we are sure that we are doing our pupils a great favour by teaching them Standard English. How can we teach our pupils if we are afraid to offend them every time we correct their mistakes?

Recently, during a training day on the teaching of A-level English, a senior examiner and exam question-setter for one of the main examination boards told a group of colleagues and myself that the idea that there is a correct way of speaking in English is something that 'we have to batter out of students'. She was surprised that pupils keep asking their English teachers about the correct way of speaking. The fact that she spoke correct Standard English must be a sign that that it was her native dialect.

In the end, we can't help transmitting our values to the next generation. Perhaps the most important value this curriculum teaches is misanthropy, in the form of cynicism towards the knowledge accumulated by humanity in the course of millennia and towards the idea that the great majority of children have the potential to acquire that knowledge; that, whatever their native dialect, they have the ability to learn academic subjects to a good level and that many will do so, given the right educational circumstances.

Nor should we blame 'our multicultural society' for our inability to devise a common curriculum. Questioning the idea of nation does not necessarily lead to fragmentation. An enthusiastic meeting of cultures in a climate of genuine tolerance can lead to a synthesis of the best that each culture has to offer. English being the international language, we are in an ideal position to devise an integrated, universal curriculum for teaching the very best that English language and literature have to offer, no matter the origin of the authors or of the pupils.

In a way, the present multicultural curriculum is motivated by a false respect for different cultures, a respect born of guilt and fear—guilt about the imperial past and fear of a future clash of civilisations. It is motivated by a dislike, or at least ambivalence and insecurity, towards British culture, rather than by a genuine interest in other cultures.

It is ironic that imperial Britain was able to integrate authors of foreign origin, such as Joseph Conrad, the Rossettis, Henry James or T.S. Eliot into the literary canon, in a way that our multicultural curriculum cannot. A poet like Derek Walcott, for instance, could probably claim his rightful place in the English canon just as much as Seamus Heaney and certainly more than the other three British poets in the *AQA Anthology*, yet he is confined to the ghetto of 'Poems from Different Cultures' together with lesser poets. The current division of poetry in English into different sections, according to the origins of the poets, serves just as much to protect native English poets from other, possibly better, poets in English, as to create a space for non-natives.

The fact that even native English citizens are seen as people belonging to different cultures, each with its own local language, shows that multiculturalism is above all in the eye of the native beholder.

## The wrong answer: a personalised curriculum

We have seen how the Cox report was ambivalent about the transmission of knowledge to the next generation, how it emphasised the dangers of cultural transmission as well as the benefits of learning Standard English and traditional English literature. Perhaps the most important response to our fear of transmitting the wrong kind of knowledge to pupils has been the adoption of a child-centred ethos by mainstream education. Unable to decide what knowledge is worth teaching the young, we have increasingly shifted the focus of education away from the object to be known (the world) and onto the learner (the self).

While the general direction of education has shifted from a subject-centred to a child-centred approach to learning (also called constructivist theory of knowledge or personalised learning), we have had over the years many 'backlashes' or 'back-to-basics' measures. These are designed to ensure that some valuable content remains, or perhaps simply to reassure public opinion: the introduction of the National Curriculum itself in 1989, the National Literacy and Numeracy Strategies in the late '90s, the adoption of phonics as a compulsory method to teach children to read in 2006. Such backlash measures are an awkward attempt to restore, in an incoherent way, isolated pieces of tradition to an education system which is based on its rejection.

So, for example, in February 2007 Mick Walters, director of the QCA, announced that the new curriculum would have 'a new focus on personal and economic well-being alongside more flexibility to incorporate a "personalised" approach to learning'.[22]

But at the same time, certainly aware of the 'dumbing down' headlines the QCA consultation paper would generate, he issued a very defensive statement which:

> sought to reassure parents and teachers that 'the well-respected and well-regarded' pillars of the curriculum would be retained: 'Anne Boleyn will still be beheaded, the Pennines will remain the backbone of England and Romeo will still fall in love with Juliet'.[23]

Education secretary Alan Johnson also felt it necessary to release a statement to reassure the public. 'There are certain untouchable elements of the secondary curriculum that all teenagers should learn for a classic, well-rounded British education. It's nonsense to claim that the curriculum is being dumbed down,'[24] he declared.

The box marked 'traditional education' will be ticked by a list of classic authors, such as Jane Austen and Charles Dickens, that have landed on teachers' desks with no apparent link to the rest of the curriculum. If we are serious about teaching children difficult literary works, we should devise a coherent system which prepares them step by step, through the study of texts of increasing difficulty from primary school to A-level.

In the end, both the modernising and the traditionalist approach are extremes of the same inability to engage with tradition in a constructive, critical way. The modernisers' attitude of rejecting the past of the 'dead white males' only for the reason that it's past is just as uncritical as the old conservative approach of preserving tradition only for the reason that things have always been done that way.

The personalised curriculum that educationalists and policy makers are now trying to devise is a response to their own inability to imagine a programme of studies for an ideal educated citizen, a curriculum that we should aspire to teach to as many children as possible, whatever their cultural or socio-economic background, in spite of the fact that we know that not everyone will reach the expected standard. Devising a personalised national curriculum—a contradiction in terms if ever there was one—is a way of getting around the difficulty of transmitting knowledge to the great majority of children. It also signals a lack of belief in the ability of the average child to benefit from an academic curriculum.

# Geography Used To Be About Maps

## Alex Standish

### Introduction

Until recently, geography has rarely been considered as a
subject for the delivery of citizenship education. While the
knowledge and skills acquired through geographic
education have often been viewed as important tools for
citizens to possess, the discussion about citizenship in
geography went little beyond this. However, since the late
1980s many geographers have begun to think of their subject
as one that can make a significant contribution to the
education of future citizens. This development coincides
with the decline of the traditional national model of
citizenship: the electorate in general, and young people in
particular, are disengaged from the traditional political
realm. Instead, people frequently seek individual rather than
social solutions to their problems.

The declining participation in a national social project is
parallelled by the rise of interest in affairs of a global nature
and alternative forms and mechanisms of 'political' action.
Thus, American geographer Sarah Bednarz asserts that: 'the
definition of citizenship may in fact be broadening from
national to international in scope'.[1] In England and Wales,
global citizenship is identified as an important aim for
pupils in the national curriculum and in some examination
syllabi. In contrast to national politics, the international
sphere appears dynamic and vibrant: the United Nations
and international non-governmental organisations being
viewed as sources of authority and positive action. At the
same time, the definition of political action has been
broadened to include personal actions, including a concern
for one's identity. Today, the expression 'the personal is

political' has become widely accepted. The post-national citizen is a cosmopolitan individual who participates in governance at different levels, such as the local community or new social movements, which are seen as more susceptible to change than traditional politics.[2] Thus, politics has become less about furthering individual and collective interest through a social project, but more about expressing concern for an 'other': the environment, other cultures, social justice for the poor.

In the notion of global citizenship many geographers have found a new niche for their subject. They have jumped on the internationalisation bandwagon and re-invented geography as a subject that teaches students about these 'new' global processes and issues. Central to this global turn has been its embrace of the 'global' ethics inherent to this new citizenship model. Students are not only being taught about how the world is, but also how it ought to be. These global values include the natural environment, cultural tolerance, social justice and equality. In global citizenship education these values transcend political and ethnic boundaries, offering a new morality based on the notion of universal human rights rather than rights tied to the nation state. Yet this chapter will show that, upon closer inspection, these values are Western in origin and frequently used to assert the interests of Western institutions or nations in the international arena.

While students are learning about global citizenship and global ethics, there has been no critical interrogation of the educational and social implications of these concepts. If an important aim of education has become the formation of the values and attitudes of students, how does this change the nature and goals of geographic education? Are values of truth and knowledge compromised by the promotion of what could be construed as a political agenda? Also, in global citizenship education pupils are treated as political subjects in their own right, capable of political action. Yet what are the consequences of blurring the distinction between adults and children? Teaching children about the world is an important prerequisite to the inheritance of political responsibility. If pupils are being treated as political subjects before they have acquired the knowledge and life experience of adults, what does this say about the nature of political action today or about adults as political subjects? It is also important to question the extent to which personal actions have political consequences. What is the relationship between personal actions and social change?

This chapter will examine the incorporation of global citizenship into the geography curriculum in England and Wales and how this has changed the nature of geographic education. The chapter concludes that there has been a shift from a focus on learning about the external world to education as an examination of the internal world of students. This is not to say that all geography teaching in England and Wales is like this. I believe there are many very competent geography teachers out there teaching excellent geography lessons. This chapter addresses the direction the subject has been moving in over the past 15 or so years, led by geographical associations, government education bodies, policy makers and some educators. There is also evidence that many teachers have welcomed the incorporation of global citizenship and its new assumptions about the nature and purpose of education.[3] Yet, in contrast to its claims to develop politically active citizens, the outcome of global citizenship education is a diminished version of the embryonic political subject, for whom social change has been reduced to the sum of personal change. Global ethics is thus focused on changing individuals, their socio-political values and personalities rather than society. As such it is an anti-democratic trend and amounts to a highly intrusive level of control by professionals and the state over individuals.

## The Rise of Global Citizenship Education

Throughout most of the twentieth century citizenship was not taught as a direct subject in England and Wales. However, as the national system of education developed there was an implicit recognition that a basic level of education was a prerequisite for participation in a liberal democracy. The system that evolved was divided between private education for the elite and public education for the masses, but nevertheless education for all as a principle had been established in the nineteenth century by individuals such as Jeremy Bentham and John Stuart Mill. In the twentieth century the national system of education became a reality with a broad based curriculum in arts, sciences and the humanities. For instance, a 1951 National Education Association Educational Policies Commission publication commented on the importance of education to the development of the individual: 'Making freely available the common heritage of human association and human culture opens to every child the opportunity to grow to his full stature'.[4] The history curriculum was the principle means through which students learnt to identify with the nation state. Students were taught about their common heritage and the history of Britain. At least this was the case until the end of the Cold War.

While the 1988 Education Reform Act made reference to citizenship education in all but name, it was only during the 1990s that government initiatives sought to make it an explicit goal of schooling. The question of citizenship was investigated by the House of Commons Speaker's Commission on Education (1990), the National Curriculum Council (1990), the Commission on Social Justice (1994) and the Citizenship Foundation (1995). Following the 1997 White Paper, *Excellence in Schools*, the Advisory Group on Citizenship was formed to make recommendations for the introduction of a citizenship curriculum for schools. Led by Professor Bernard Crick, the advisory group described its rational for mandating citizenship education in schools:

> It can no longer sensibly be left as uncoordinated local initiatives which vary greatly in number, content and method. This is an inadequate basis for animating the idea of a common citizenship with democratic values.[5]

This is an explicit recognition that the social structures that used to organically engage people in community or national issues are no longer playing that function. The dismissive attitude of young people towards traditional politics has been the subject of several reports.[6]

The goal of the Advisory Group on Citizenship was no less than to change the 'political culture' of the country and to enact a 'shift of emphasis between, on the one hand, state welfare provision and responsibility and, on the other, community and individual responsibility'.[7] In actuality, this shift in responsibility is about the state taking a direct role in ensuring that young people have 'socially responsible' attitudes and behaviours, leaving young people less responsibility for making their own decisions about such matters.

In September 2000, citizenship education became part of the national curriculum for English and Welsh primary schools. In September 2002, citizenship education was mandated as a separate discipline for secondary schools implementing many of the Crick Report's recommendations. Although citizenship was outlined as an independent subject, aware of the time pressures on teachers to meet growing statutory teaching demands, the Crick Report emphasised links to other curricula areas especially history, geography, English and Personal, Social and Health

Education (PSHE). While knowledge about government, politics and British history were included, so were personal values and dispositions, community involvement, practicing democracy and global citizenship. These latter elements and the emphasis on PSHE, geography and English, not traditionally subjects associated with citizenship education, are indicative of a new approach to citizenship education and one that is no longer tied to the nation state.

In the citizenship national curriculum document teachers are required to teach pupils about how the United Kingdom is governed and how they should contribute to the national democratic process. However, the nation is presented as just one scale at which politics is conducted along a continuum from local to global. For instance, at Key Stage 2 pupils are encouraged to 'develop their sense of social justice and moral responsibility and begin to understand that their own choices and behaviour can affect local, national or global issues and political and social institutions'.[8] Once the nation becomes one of several levels at which politics gets conducted it loses its uniqueness. Hence, it has been argued that individuals today demonstrate identities existing at different levels rather than an over-riding commitment to the nation state.[9] Other parts of the citizenship national curriculum explicitly emphasise the global scale. At Key Stage 3, teachers are instructed to teach pupils about: 'The world as a global community, and the political, economic, environmental and social implications of this, and the role of the European Union, the Commonwealth and the United Nations'.[10]

Against a backdrop of falling numbers taking the subject in both schools and universities during the 1990s, some members of the geography community began promoting the subject as one that could deliver global citizenship, embracing issues of environmentalism, sustainability, human rights, equality, democracy and social justice.[11] In

1992, the International Charter on Geographical Education proposed that through geography pupils should develop attitudes and values conducive to a 'concern for the quality of the environment, respect for rights of all people to equality, and dedication to seeking solutions to human problems'.[12] In April 1999 the Geographical Association released a new position statement, which set out a new ethically engaged role for geography. Their aims for geography included developing an informed concern for the world around us and an ability and willingness to take positive action, both locally and globally.[13] Similarly, the revised Geography National Curriculum launched in September 2000 highlighted four important elements: sustainable development, global citizenship, values and attitudes and location knowledge (Department for Education and Employment/Qualifications and Curriculum Authority, 1999).

In 2002, the Geovisions Working Group of the Geographical Association began work on a new 'hybrid' GCSE geography course. One of its aims was described as to 'promote global citizenship by leading towards awareness and understanding of global systems, global patterns, the processes and impacts of globalisation and the opportunities and responsibilities of the individual'.[14] This new GCSE is promoted as more relevant to pupils and is now being used in a number of schools in the country. Its emphasis upon the personal ethics of pupils is apparent in its specification of content document: 'Candidates should be encouraged to examine their own values as they analyse the values of others and to become aware of the power relations implicit in any situation and the conflicts and inequalities which may arise'.[15]

Environmentalism is a central theme for global citizenship. Both environmental education and education for sustainable development have played roles in the elevation of environmental values in the curriculum.[16] Since the 1987 World Commission on Sustainable Development and the 1992 Earth Summit in Rio de Janeiro, the concept of sustainability has gained social credence. Agenda 21, the report from the Earth Summit, recommended that governments make 'a thorough review of curricula... to ensure that there is a multidisciplinary approach which encompasses environment and development issues; ... that every school should be assisted in designing environmental activity work plans'.[17] Indeed, the citizenship national curriculum document specifies at Key Stage 4 that pupils should be taught about 'the wider issues and challenges of global interdependence and responsibility, including sustainable development and Local Agenda 21'.[18] The inclusion of environmental values amounts to an educational approach that emphasises the value of the natural environment for reasons other than instrumental or aesthetic purpose. Environmental values reflect a shift in emphasis away from an anthropocentric approach to society and management of natural resources towards an approach that is sceptical of the righteousness and capacity of humans to intervene in or manage ecosystems. Instead, intrinsic value or authority over human endeavour is given to natural systems.

Geography textbooks and other examination boards in England and Wales have also appropriated the concepts of global citizenship and sustainable development. London's main examination board Edexcel has dedicated large sections of its geography GCSE syllabus to 'managing the environment'.[19] The Assessment and Qualification Alliance makes reference to 'an appreciation of the environment' and 'an understanding of global citizenship' in their aims for GCSE geography.[20] Exam questions might ask pupils, for example, to detail a sustainable approach to tourism. Pupils are expected to consider their own responsibility for global issues in the Advanced Level geography textbook *Global*

*Challenge,*[21] including the over-consumption of resources, high fertility rates and growing numbers of refugees. In earlier geography textbooks social, economic and political processes were portrayed as something that was addressed though the nation state and its political framework. Yet today, the elevation of governance at multiple scales over national government has prompted some geographers to call for geography textbooks to move beyond state-centrism.[22]

The Nuffield Foundation, a UK charitable trust, also makes a point of the links between geography and the new citizenship:

> Knowledge and understanding of human behaviour, its consequences for other humans and the world they inhabit, are indisputably important to all students in a healthy democracy. The same can be said about the development of the political, social and ethical values which guide their behaviour.[23]

What the Foundation fails to address, however, is that there is no world system of democracy and hence no formal mechanisms for citizens to shape politics beyond the confines of their nation state.

While the idea of global citizenship is not new, the argument being put forth here is that it has grown in significance since the late 1980s. For example, after the Second World War, when there was interest in global education, a 1974 UNESCO conference led to the publication of 'Recommendations Concerning Education for International Understanding, Co-operation and Peace and Education relating to Human Rights and Fundamental Freedom'. The conference viewed geographic education as a subject that promotes 'understanding, tolerance and friendship amongst all nations, racial and religious groups and furthers the activities of the United Nations for the maintenance of peace'.[24] Nevertheless, the movement for global education and global citizenship remained peripheral to mainstream education in a world dominated by the interaction of nation-states and Cold War divisions. It was only as the world moved into the post-Cold War political framework that social issues were increasingly viewed in global terms and the education system, as a vehicle for cultural transmission, has engaged in a concerted attempt to shape a new generation versed in global issues.[25] Global change education is thus a burgeoning field beyond England and Wales and in other disciplines.[26]

At a summit meeting in Charlottesville in 1989, leading Americans expressed concern about the decline in domestic manufacturing, loss of competitiveness, a relative decline in living standards and a sense that America was struggling to remain on top of the global pile. Wilbanks reports that there was a general sense these problems had 'something to do with connectivity'.[27] One outcome of the summit was the inclusion of a previously neglected geography curriculum as one of five core subjects in the 1994 'Goals 2000: Educate America Act'. Indeed, since this time geography has experienced something of a renaissance in American education, although it still well behind history in terms of the number of students taking the subject in schools and colleges. Sarah Bednarz has outlined the role of geographic education in shaping citizens in a post-9/11 America. She argues that geography is in a new position of 'preparing participatory citizens' and that through service-learning pupils will develop a 'vision of citizenship as personal responsibility'.[28] Service-learning means tying education to work in the community. Also, it is not just geography that is embracing the themes of global citizenship education. In the past few years, many schools, colleges and universities have launched initiatives in global or international education.

The recent promotion of global citizenship has mirrored the declining attachment to the nation state, traditional politics and pupil interest in civics and history. Ravitch and Viteritti[29] suggest that the 1990s was the decade when scholars of civic education questioned the condition of democracy. The end of the Cold War marked the conclusion of the political contestation between competing visions of social organisation. With capitalism as the only surviving social model, it has struggled to offer any sense of social progress. When nations lack a sense of historical progress it should come as no surprise that the up-and-coming generation, lacking a strong sense of attachment to common goals, does not seek political solutions to their problems, but instead resorts to individual survival mechanisms. In American schools, the unpopularity of traditional citizenship classes and the poor grasp that students have of the foundations of American democracy is well documented.[30] A 1999 US Department of Education survey revealed that only 20 per cent of youths have a proficient understanding of the US constitution and the principles underlying government.[31]

A main attraction of global citizenship education is its elevation of the individual over states, inherent in the notion of universal human rights.[32] While national citizenship is seen as promoting division, global citizenship portrays all as equal, thus enhancing unity. Because geography is a field of knowledge rather than a discrete discipline with clear boundaries, such as physics for example, it has always tended to be a more malleable subject.[33] In the nineteenth and early twentieth centuries it was dominated by the physical sciences, stressing the determinacy of the natural environment upon human behaviour. Human geography grew within the subject as the twentieth century evolved and people began to place greater emphasis on human agency and how people shape their environment. Hence, the subject, perhaps more than most, reflects the prevailing social ideas at any historical moment. In the nineteenth century geography was almost synonymous with Empire in the British context. With the collapse of Empire, development and national sovereignty were important themes.

Today, the themes of globalisation and interdependence between localities are dominant. It is also a spatial subject that seeks to make links between different scales and between the human and the natural world; hence its suitability to the themes of global citizenship. The proposition 'think global, act local,' has been adopted by some geographers as a way of encouraging students to take on responsibility for global issues.

However, rather than teaching pupils about the world so that they can decide the most appropriate course of action, global citizenship education is tied to specific non-academic values that tend towards the replacement of knowledge with morality as the central focus of the curriculum. Thus global problems are not presented as issues to be interrogated for truth, knowledge and meaning, with a view to students developing ideas about the potential courses of social and political action. Instead, the solution is to be found in the personal realm and is presented as a given: that people need to adhere to a new global values system that encourages them to consume less, have fewer children, take public transport rather than drive their cars, be less money-grabbing, support charities, and so forth. Such an approach is no substitute for educating pupils to interpret the world for themselves. This anti-intellectual and anti-democratic nature of global citizenship education will be explained further in the following section.

If the aims of geographical education are changing, then it is understandable that new teaching methods are proposed to deliver ethics education. Traditional 'chalk and talk' or lecturing is derided as too teacher-centred and criticised for its 'passive' approach to learning. Critics suggest that because students are given the answers they do not learn to think for themselves. Instead, several methods are proposed as leading to more 'meaningful' learning. Enquiry-based learning or problem-solving are recommended because they encourage pupils to take some control over their own learning. Pupils help to define the problem, the questions that need to be answered and how they will go about their research. The teacher is seen as a facilitator who guides students through their learning.

Another approach associated with citizenship education is service-learning or community-based learning. Dorsey[34] advocates this approach for undergraduates because it makes direct links between the community and university. It also gives pupils the opportunity to make links between theory and practice and to experience 'doing citizenship'. With both of these methods it is suggested that doing rather than listening results in better memory retention. However, there is little evidence to suggest a link between volunteering or helping with a school project and political engagement as an adult. Both enquiry-based and service-learning reject abstract ideas as a prelude to political thought. Again, how are young people going to act in and shape the world if they do not understand complex contemporary political issues and how the system works? At least the national model of citizenship education taught students about the political system and the principles and mechanisms of civic engagement.

### What is different about global citizenship education?

Global citizenship education differs from previous national models of liberal education—and not just in scale. In the early decades of the twentieth century the progressive movement promoted the idea of education as scientific endeavour that should be free from moral instruction. In particular, John Dewey emphasised 'the independence of the child for the purposes of liberating children to develop socially, intellectually and morally'.[35] This progressive turn influenced education throughout the Western world. In

England and Wales the church continued to play a role with respect to education—one that would be considered unacceptable in many Western nations. However, an important principle had been established as far as subjects were concerned, that of respect for individuals' freedom of conscience and their right to determine their own social and political value systems. Hence, for much of the post-war period most disciplines have held back from explicitly promoting political or non-academic values. Scientific enquiry was about the pursuit of truth, which was understood to be a non-moral issue.[36]

This principle was not always upheld in practice. In particular, the history curriculum should and has been criticised for its nationalistic bias and attempt to instil patriotic values in pupils, for example, the fixation on the Second World War and how the Allies defeated the Nazis, while downplaying more embarrassing episodes such as the Boer War. Requiring pupils to commit themselves to a particular set of values was always open to criticism of political bias in education systems that held academic principles of truth, rationality, objectivity and scientific evidence as it cornerstones. This all changed in the 1990s, with the cultural/moral turn of the social sciences that has challenged these foundations of liberalism. The national education system was at least built on the notion of pupils as embryonic political subjects who would grow up to take an active part in shaping public life. In contrast, global citizenship education starts from the assumption of a degraded embryonic political subject who is disengaged from public life and is not going to evolve into a politically active body of its own accord.

Drawing on the ideas of Foucault and other post-structuralist philosophers, many social theorists have argued that all knowledge is socially constructed in particular contexts and hence is non-transferable from one locality or social situation to the next. Foucault argued that it was only through knowledge and discourse that objects attained meaning.[37] Thus, for Foucault, knowledge of the material world is a social construction and specific to the social group who produced it. Here knowledge is situated and coloured by the particular values of those who 'produced' it. Foucault concluded that outside of this context knowledge was meaningless.

In post-structuralism, truth is replaced by truths and knowledge by knowledges. Thus, much of our present inherited knowledge is dismissed as only one perspective: that of a Western, white, male, middle-class elite. If knowledge can no longer be abstracted from the particular social context in which it arose, it cannot be separated from the prejudices or values of the individual who constructed it. In this sense post-structuralism holds a limited social interpretation of knowledge. All knowledge is viewed as political or biased and thus truth no longer holds its non-moral status. All knowledge then becomes a moral battle-ground.

Furthermore, Foucault asserted that knowledge or discourse was used by the state to exercise control and power over the rest of society.[38] Education was one institution that Foucault saw as a key to the discourse of elite control. Through education, acceptable and unacceptable behaviours and ideas were championed. While it is true that the state does seek to regulate social behaviour and aspects of knowledge, Foucault fails to make a distinction between the form and content of knowledge. Is knowledge itself the problem or the way that it is used?

Smith[39] documents the rise of 'moral geographies' in the 1990s, although he traces its origins back to the 'radical' or 'humanist' geographers of the 1970s and 1980s, in particular the work of Harvey and Tuan. In 1991, the Social and Cultural Geography Study Group of the Institute of British

Geographers called for geographers to engage with ethics, involving 'the articulation of the moral and the spatial'.[40] A few years later, a session at the 1994 Association of American Geographers conference entitled 'Rethinking Metatheory: Ethics, Difference and Universals' furthered the rise of moral issues in geography.

Some geographers have seized upon Foucault's ideas of socially constructed knowledge and the power of discourse to examine the role of education in the constitution of subjects. Drawing on psychoanalytic and post-structural theory, Laclau has developed the idea of politics as identity forming. As Rasmussen and Brown explain, 'Politics is not about defending the intrinsic interests of a political subject but about a struggle to construct subjects, making identity a primary ground for the operation of politics'.[41]

The idea that educators should be agents of social change has been expressed in several forms: 'transformative geography' encourages students to 'practice the discipline of geography for the well-being of people and the environment';[42] 'feminist pedagogy', where education is 'a fluid process whereby the student is empowered to act for social change';[43] 'active social science' which presents geography as 'a means for social ends such as progress and problem solving';[44] political geography, such as taking a 'pro-environmental position';[45] combining geography with peace studies;[46] and citizenship education in which the geographically informed citizen is 'a person who can think about this need to be vigilant about their rights and duties'.[47] While the rhetoric of these ideas appears radical and progressive, in that they seek to treat pupils as active subjects of social and political change, what is obscured is a sleight of hand by which, in each of the above examples, 'social' and 'political' change has been reduced to changing the individual.

A couple of examples from common geography lessons will hopefully help to clarify this shift from a concern with learning about the outside world to the values and attitudes individuals harbour. A common task in geography text-books today is to ask students to evaluate their own environmental impact. This might be in relation to con-sumption of material goods or production of carbon emissions. While students are not *directly* instructed what to think about the environment, the activity demands that students examine their personal values and behaviour and rests on the presumption that lowering one's environmental impact is a positive development. The goal then becomes for students to become more aware of their consumption habits, taking into account the environmental impact of what they buy. Here, personal actions have become entirely imbued with political outcomes and an examination of the personal realm has replaced learning about environmental issues in a social and political context. In contrast, a political discussion about the environment would examine the benefits to people of resource utilisation versus which parts of the environment we would choose to conserve. In other words, it would situate the discussion in terms of what is best for different sections of society or society in general. Knowledge of the politics of environmental decisions would be something students could draw upon as adults when such issues arise. The point is these are social decisions, necessitating societal actions, not individual actions. Removing them from their social context means that political issues have been replaced with moral ones.

A second example is fair trade, a topic that is broached in many geography curricula today. Pupils are presented with information about the relative costs of buying 'normal' products versus 'fair trade' goods and who gets what in the production supply chain. With fair trade goods the farmers receive an incrementally improved return on their primary product. Again, pupils are not necessarily told what to think, but the information presented is unlikely to lead one to question the merits of fair trade and the outcome again is to encourage students to scrutinise their consumption patterns. However, the issue is again presented to students in simplistic, narrow and personal terms. There is no evaluation of why a farmer is entirely dependent upon the market value of primary commodities for survival and how that circumstance could be altered through development, which could transform their productivity, diversify their production and achieve a higher market price, as is the case in the First World. Again, the issue has been removed from its wider social and political context making it solely a matter of individual consciousness.

With the politics of identity, the human subject is viewed in a more restricted role. The stage on which individuals conduct 'politics' and take action is identity itself. Here, decisions, actions, and knowledge are all concerned with the development of the self. Within the parameters set by global ethics, individuals are encouraged to become more conscious of the forces that shape identity. By restricting subjectivity to a concern with the psyche rather than social change, theorists have opened up the possibility for children to be viewed as subjects in their own right. The notion of children as holders of rights has grown in significance since the 1989 United Nations Convention on the Rights of the Child asserted that the child is 'no longer the passive recipient of benefits, the child has become the subject or holder of rights'.[48] There is an expanding literature on 'children's geographies' including a new journal dedicated to the topic that explores the lives of children, their understanding of the world and seeks to empower them as 'active citizens'.[49] Including pupils in the development of their own curriculum has been suggested by Simon Catling.[50] Writing in the journal *Geography*, Catling argues for a child-centred curriculum which advocates 'working with children as participants, partners and responsible members of the local and global community'.[51] In these examples, 'empowering' or 'working with children' mean more than providing pupils with knowledge about the world. Rather, educators are seeking to engage pupils in a discussion about global ethics.

The concern for the individual psyche of pupils is often explicit in the curriculum, not just embedded within the promotion of socio-political values. In the English National Curriculum for Citizenship Key Stage 2 pupils are taught 'to recognise, as they approach puberty, how people's emotions change at that time and how to deal with their feelings towards themselves, their family and others in a positive way'; while at Key Stages 3 and 4 pupils are taught to 'reflect on the process of participating'.[52]

Geography's acceptance of post-structuralist assumptions about the foundations of knowledge has facilitated its acceptance of global citizenship education, global ethics and identity as worthy educational goals. In particular, taking post-structuralist assumptions about the socially particular nature of education, geographers have challenged the previously held ideas about the boundaries of education. Abandoning the values of common truth, knowledge and the privacy of individual conscience, post-structuralist geographers have re-focused education on the moral development of the individual at the expense of their intellectual development. While advocates of global citizenship education claim that they do not instil their socio-political values in pupils, there is clearly an expectation that pupils will embrace global ethics: that they will stand up for environmental values, defend the poor against the 'injustices' of capitalism and be tolerant of other cultures. Where lessons about the geography of the world have been replaced by an examination of 'global issues', not only are pupils being deprived of the descriptive and explanatory power of learning about the world, but they are being encouraged to think in a particular way that conforms to contemporary moral diktats and expresses a misanthropic worldview. Here, social change has been reduced to changing the individual. Unfortunately, a full exploration of the nature of global ethics and their negative interpretation of humanity is beyond the scope of this chapter. However, the diminished political subject presupposed in global citizenship education will be analysed in the next section.

## The degraded embryonic political subject of global citizenship education

The aspiration for a global society consisting of politically motivated cosmopolitan subjects contributing to a central democratic system of government is a positive vision to uphold and helps to explain the appeal of global citizenship education. Unfortunately, closer inspection of global citizenship education reveals that this vision is far from the reality of what is currently on offer. Conversely, the global citizen in global citizenship education is a diminished version of a political subject, who ascribes to global ethics rather than their own moral compass. This unhappy transformation is the outcome of the rejection of the national framework for politics by a middle-class elite, rather than its transcendence by a mass political movement. The elevation and conflation of the local and the global in the proposition 'Think global, act local' is implicitly a rejection of the national sphere. It represents a denial of the political system through which citizens currently express their collective will via political representatives: the national will as sovereign power in the international sphere. Therefore, not only is global citizenship disingenuous with regard to how the world currently operates (there is no world government, nor global body for citizens to hold to account), it is rejecting collective interest as a means through which politics is conducted while offering no democratic alternative. This is not to say that the national system of politics was without problems, but at least it rested upon the notion of autonomous subjects. In contrast, global citizenship education seeks to usurp traditional politics with the politics of identity, whereby 'subjects' are expected to conform to its global ethics. In doing so, global citizenship education has reinvented the meanings of citizenship, politics and the political subject.

Children are not political subjects with political rights because they don't have the intellectual capabilities and experience to comprehend complex political processes and ideas. Nevertheless, global citizenship education aims to treat children as political subjects in their own right. This is possible only because global citizenship education has changed the meaning of politics from social change to a concern with identity. Here the meaning of politics has become the actual constitution of the subject or the embryonic subject in the case of pupils. With global citizenship education politics has become less about preparing pupils for participation in the public process of allocating society's resources and more about influencing several aspects of pupils' fundamental value systems that shape personality and identity. In the words of Mitchell, nurturing cosmopolitan citizens is about 'the constitution of subjects orientated to individual survival and/or success in the global economy'.[53] Identity formation has become the purposeful political act rather than the social action, with schools playing a key role in shaping the pupil's identity.

Global citizenship education seeks to influence the identity of pupils because it starts from the premise of an individual of diminished capacity. Proponents of global citizenship education presume that people are not evolving into political subjects through the acquisition of knowledge and skills alone. This leaves them potentially detached from public life and a meaningful relationship to the state. As noted by political theorist Vanessa Pupavac: 'the children's rights discourse, premised on the incompetency of the child, challenges the assumption that the rights-bearing individual is competent' and, 'calls into question the existence of the rational, autonomous individual'.[54]

The very idea of children's incompetence elevates the need for advocacy on behalf of the child. That the state and professionals are promoting global citizenship education calls into question the legitimacy and capacity of parents to undertake such a task. Again, the point is well made by Pupavac: 'Children's rights empower professionals to act in the name of the child and undermine the right of the individual citizens to decide how to bring up their children.'[55]

Therefore, global citizenship education degrades both young people as embryonic political subjects and adults as independent political subjects. It presumes that neither is capable of acting as an independent moral agent by blurring the boundaries between the political world of adults and the world of children.[56] Children can be presented as political subjects because following global ethics has replaced real political responsibility. Children and adults alike can participate in the 'politics' of global ethics because no independent thought or understanding is required.

Starting from a presumption of incompetence and vulnerability of individuals allows the state to step in and play a paternalistic or therapeutic role with regard to the private conscience of the individual. The Crick Report[57] was quite explicit on this point that global citizenship education seeks to reconstitute the relationship between the state and individual through socially sanctioned organisational bodies.

This changes the goals of education. Rather than learning about the world around us, so that young people can comprehend it and decide how they wish to engage with it, global ethics education teaches pupils about their own values system and how to live their lives. The proposition 'Think global, act local' only demands that individuals consider their personal attitudes and how their actions influence larger processes such as global warming or over-consumption. It teaches pupils that there are larger forces that cannot be controlled, so they must modify their actions accordingly. When the question of what action to take arises in global citizenship education, only individual or limited social actions are encouraged, like clearing a neighbourhood of rubbish or donating to a campaign for human rights. The purpose of such actions only serves to make the individual feel better about themselves, rather than bring about meaningful change. The same is true for the ethics of human rights, democracy, peace or cultural tolerance. They are concerned with the individual state of being, as opposed to asserting political rights or self-interest. Frequently, the focus on human rights and other cultures requires that pupils empathise with other people and cultures through an understanding of their lives. Furedi[58] observes how education has moved towards therapeutic rather than intellectual goals. He describes how teachers are encouraged to help pupils feel better about themselves, have a positive self-image, and how to feel and respond to events in a 'positive' manner.

This process of engagement with the private world of individual pupils has been termed 'deep citizenship' by some proponents. Machon and Walkington describe deep citizenship as a process that 'establishes links between public and private actions so that the personal or particular decision making takes into account universal concerns— indeed they become one'.[59] The consequence of blurring the distinction between the private and public world of individuals is to confuse the meaning and significance of personal actions. Global ethics seeks to impact and regulate personal actions. However, the demands of global ethics are not a positive endorsement of the capacity of people to change the world for the better. They mystify the relationship between action and social change. Because personal actions will not transform the world they are most likely to lead to further disillusionment with the potential of people to change the world for the better, encouraging further calls for restraint on human endeavour.

While the rhetoric of individual identity formation appears radical and progressive in that it elevates the role of the individual in shaping identity, it downplays the purposeful social actions from which identity is derived, avoiding the issue of collective action for political change. As Chandler observes, activism loses any sense of purpose in the absence of collective aspiration for change: 'Without a prior relationship of collective aspirations and engagement, individual activism loses any sense of collective meaning'.[60] Political action that can result in meaningful social change comes from citizens who express a common purpose and exercise their political right to bring that change about. In global citizenship education pupils are pressed to re-evaluate their personal values and identity in response to contemporary social issues. While ultimately it is true that pupils can reject global values, these lessons reinforce a strong moral imperative that permeates society rather than offering critical analysis. Few pupils on their own would argue against environmental values or question the logic of cultural tolerance. This has changed the aims and nature of education to a focus on the identity of pupils. Yet, if the personal consciousness of individuals is no longer a place of freedom in education, then they are no longer free moral beings. In global citizenship education the rights-bearing subject is replaced with one who needs 'guidance' to make social and political decisions. As such it amounts to the abandonment of democratic social change and its replacement with a new insidious morality.

Not only does global citizenship education abandon the concept of democratic social change, it reinforces a hegemonic power structure. In many ways, the global agenda represents the inability of elites to cohere a national project. Instead, Western national interests are being asserted through the language of global ethics and empowerment. Global citizenship disguises these national interests as universal norms or morals to which all should adhere. Ironically, this agenda often appears to be one that is radical and anti-establishment, frequently being promoted by nongovernmental organisations (NGOs) or by anti-globalisation protesters, seeking to empower under-represented or marginalised peoples.[61] However, Chandler[62] notes that despite the radical image NGOs and anti-globalisation protesters like to present, they are very much in cahoots with elite organisations of society such as the United Nations, the International Monetary Fund and the World Bank, which also promote the causes of human rights, environmentalism, cultural sensitivity and democracy. NGOs are predominantly funded through Western international bodies, such as the European Union, and anti-globalisation protesters are frequently hired by Western corporations to advise on policies of cultural and environmental sensitivity. The links between humanitarianism and Western intervention have been well documented by Chandler and Duffield.[63] It is important to recall that the second Gulf War was launched in the name of the 'human rights' of the Iraqi people and was seeking to 'democratise' Iraq (among other reasons cited). Global ethics of environmentalism, cultural tolerance, social justice and equality in recent times, then, are Western inventions and peddled by Western institutions.

Furthermore, the role of government itself in the promotion of global citizenship education itself should not be underestimated. In both the US and England, the past decade has seen an unprecedented level of intervention into the affairs of schools. It might appear that rising government influence over the curriculum in the form of a national curriculum or national standards and its promotion of global citizenship education would be a contradiction. However, this illustrates not only the emphasis that government is placing on schools to address social issues, but that global ethics are not so global after all. Today, Western governments seeking to assert national interest appeal to global ethics and universal human rights.

In the absence of any link between personal values and social change, the only active agent capable of change in the global ethics agenda, concludes Chandler, is a higher authority such as NGOs, intergovernmental organisations like the United Nations or government itself. Hence, global citizenship education teaches deference to these Western institutions and consequently reinforces a Western agenda on the South.

Through the language of empowerment and identity formation, global citizenship education replaces the political process with a new moral code and encourages deference to higher authority rather than independent political thought. Global citizenship education can present its project as one of political empowerment because it has changed the meaning of politics.

In this sense, global citizenship education is a political project that undermines fundamental tenets of liberalism, rejecting pupils as embryonic political subjects who will become independent political subjects through the acquisition of knowledge. This is a diminished conception of the potential of individuals to change their world for the better. Responsibility for social change is not presented as something that young people will inherit; instead they are shown how to think and act 'responsibly'. To the extent that these notions are accepted, people have given up on democratic social change. The abandonment of the collective expression of political subjects is simultaneously an abandonment of the individual subject.

## Resuscitating the embryonic political subject

The corollary of the problem with global citizenship education is its rejection of a common framework of human experience and knowledge, resulting in the endowment of individual actions with political meaning. Yet, there is a glaring contradiction in the differential approach taken in global citizenship education towards morality and knowledge. Morality is given a universal quality while simultaneously denying the possibility that knowledge can be transferred from one context to the next. As Hammersley observes in a discussion of research goals:

> Where, previously, ethical considerations were believed to set boundaries to what researchers could do in pursuit of knowledge, now ethical considerations are treated by some as constituting the very rationale of research... the possibility and perhaps desirability of knowledge have come to be downplayed by instrumentalism and postmodernism (and) a concern for ethics has expanded to fill the space.[64]

Yet how can those promoting an advocacy approach to education be confident in their ethical claims if they cannot be confident in knowledge? Veck[65] realised this flaw. In his aspiration for 'emancipatory research' Veck concluded: 'In committing to social justice I was logically bound to the pursuit of truth. If the outcome of my research was to uncover injustice, to pronounce what was wrong, then what

I had to say had to reflect the reality of that social injustice with the utmost accuracy'.[66]

To resuscitate the embryonic political subject means moving beyond the post-structuralist notion of situated and socially constructed knowledge in social theory and education. While there is always a subjective element to knowledge this does not mean that it cannot be abstracted from one context to the next. Only by recognising the common experiences and insights of people from other cultures can young people learn that ideas make sense in very different social contexts. To achieve this realisation, young people need to be taught about other parts of the world and other cultures, but not through identity politics or by practicing empathy. The politics of identity emphasises our past and presents a limited role for our capacity to shape our world. In its search for difference between cultures that is precisely what it finds: different cultures. Rather, pupils need to be taught about the common struggle that people from different places face, despite differences. They need to learn to see people rather than culture in order to recognise our common humanity and people as the agents of change.

Such learning only comes from a comprehensive education that offers pupils not only knowledge about the world but a theoretical and conceptual framework through which they can situate ideas. This framework is sorely lacking in many geography textbooks today. Furthermore, pupils can, and should, engage in mock political debates and learn about the application of knowledge to social and political issues. When ideas are tested in a social context, people are forced to back them up with evidence and logic, sorting the chaff from the grain. Only in the pursuit of truth does social justice become a possibility and can social and political theory offer meaning to pupils beyond institutional walls. Combined, these educational experiences will provide young people with the essential intellectual and social tools that will enable them to assume political responsibility as adults. These changes to education and social theory are essential for young people to be able to make sense of the world and begin to recognise the historical role that confronts them once they inherit political responsibility as adults.

## Conclusion

The dismissal of the political subject in global citizenship education is evident in its rejection of the right of nations to sovereign determination and the right of individuals to privacy of conscience and to determine their own political system of values. Global ethics are used to assert Western national interests on the international stage at the expense of Southern nations. Using the language of human rights, democracy or overpopulation, Western nations have intervened in Kosovo, Afghanistan and India. Examples of intervention on environmental grounds include demands for a reduction of greenhouse gas emissions, conservation of rainforests and protests about the construction of dams. In the post-Second World War era, countries were able to rid themselves of the shackles of colonial rule and determine their own futures. They are now losing this very same sovereignty in the name of global citizenship. This is not being done in an old fashioned nationalistic colonial project. Instead, non-governmental organisations, professionals and educators lay the groundwork for intervention. Global citizenship education teaches students that Western intervention in the South is a positive process.

At the level of the individual subject, the intrusive content and implications of global ethics should not be underestimated. The private consciousness of individual pupils is targeted, seeking to redirect their thoughts about non-academic and political values and attitudes. It is even assumed that this is a positive process because advocates presume that individuals are not capable of determining their own moral framework or at least the one that is being proposed. Furedi[67] questions the wisdom of asking teachers to broach therapeutic concerns when they are not trained in this area and concludes that engaging pupils' feelings and personal responses is far more intrusive than controlling their behaviour.

If educators no longer seek to equip their pupils with 'knowledge and literature' as Jefferson envisaged, then how can they become moral agents capable of political action? But this is the point. Global citizenship education is about acquiescence to a passive version of a political subject, for both adults and children, and a geopolitical status quo that reinforces global injustice. The focus on personal change is indicative of the abandonment of the possibility for social change that is inherent in global citizenship education. The rejection of the collective and the individual subjects are linked and expressed in the abandonment of the politics of the nation state and individuals as independent moral agents. Not only are citizens being redefined in passive terms, but young people are being denied access to a common curriculum that can offer them insight into the social and natural world around them. This is an anti-democratic trend indeed.

# The New History Boys

# Chris McGovern

What should pupils learn in their history lessons? It depends, of course, on how history, as a school subject, is defined. Until around 40 years ago it was fairly universally regarded as an unfolding narrative of the past. Then came the revolution. With an increasing number of subjects clamouring for curriculum time, many history teachers lost their nerve and, worse, appeared to lose faith in their subject. A 1968 article in the journal of the Historical Association even went so far as to suggest that there was 'a real danger of history disappearing from the time-table as a subject in its own right'.[1]

History would have to be redefined, repackaged and re-established as something rather different if it was going to justify its existence and to survive in the classroom. Never mind the collective wisdom of hundreds, even thousands, of years of history teaching. This would have to be ditched in the name of 'progress' and of 'relevance'. There was an easy solution. Rather than improving the quality of teaching, and this may have been necessary, the chosen pathway was to change the subject, to teach something else but under a re-branded name—'New History'.

The revolution was spearheaded by a quango called the Schools Council. In 1972 it set up a 'History 13-16 Project', with the specific objective of redefining the subject in a utilitarian way in order to justify its place in the curriculum since 'old subjects, such as history, must inevitably justify their continued existence'.[2] The so-called New History would focus on 'skills' such as the evaluation of evidence and the ability to empathise with people in the past. It would also teach concepts such as 'causation' and

'motivation', 'change' and 'continuity'. This redefined, utilitarian history would make it 'a suitable study for
adolescents in school'.[3] Central to this revolution would be
the dogma that 'history is not a body of knowledge
structured on either chronology or any other conceptual
framework' but, rather, 'a heap of materials which survives
from the past...'[4] In other words, the subject could only be
'saved' by ditching the one element that makes the subject
unique – that it is a coherent body of knowledge.

The revolution has been successful. The Schools Council
History 13-16 Project has evolved into the Schools History
Project (SHP). Over a third of candidates for GCSE history
sit papers on the SHP syllabus. More importantly, the New
History has taken over the entire curriculum and examining
system for history and has been enshrined in law since the
National Curriculum was introduced in 1988.

Within the profession genuine debate about the
revolution has now, largely, ceased. In the maintained sector
the price to pay for dissent has been loss of livelihood.[5]
Entry to teacher training in the subject might as well be
based on an oath of loyalty to New History, such is its
stranglehold. Within the educational world debate is, at best,
stifled. Even the Royal Society of Arts (RSA) has succumbed.
Its 2007 lecture series on 'Teaching History', chaired by the
BBC's Greg Neale, was, at times, a parody of meaningful
discussion.[6] At the second of three sessions the guest
speaker, a Cambridge don, informed her audience that: 'I
have to confess that I do not know the ins and outs of the
actual history curriculum'. Small surprise, then, that she
could not comprehend why her Cambridge undergraduates
seemed to lack historical knowledge:

> You know, most of my students don't know who the Black and
> Tans are (*sic*) so when I taught 'Juno and the Paycock' last term I
> had to, you know, I had to explain to them the very basics of, you
> know, England's relationship with Ireland.

The series culminated in a 'discussion' in which the five invited speakers largely agreed amongst themselves. At least the fifth and last speaker, Labour MP Gordon Marsden, recognised this when he said that: 'We obviously needed David Starkey here this evening' (derisory laughter).

How has the New History revolution affected the way in which our children are taught? We are forever being reassured by educational professionals and by Government ministers that all is well with National Curriculum history. We are told that British history is central, knowledge important and chronological understanding secure. But is it? From time to time the media publishes surveys of the public's knowledge of the past—especially Britain's past. The results, invariably, reveal a quite stunning ignorance, especially amongst the younger generation—the 'beneficiaries' of New History teaching in our schools. In August 2004, for example, prior to the launch of its 'Battlefield Britain' series, the BBC issued a press release headed: 'Alexander the Great won the Battle of Hastings ... Gandalf defeated the Spanish Armada ... the Battle of Britain was a key turning point in the Hundred Years War ... the Romans never invaded Britain ...'[7] It went on to explain that a survey it had commissioned on knowledge of landmark events in British history revealed 'the older generations are far more clued up on their history than the supposedly sharper 16 to 44 age groups'. Amongst 16-34 year-olds a third could not spot the victor in the Battle of Hastings from these five options:

a) Napoleon
b) Wellington
c) Alexander the Great
d) William the Conqueror
e) Don't know

Half of this younger age group did not know the Battle of Britain happened during World War II and almost a half could not connect Sir Francis Drake to the battle against the Spanish Armada, naming, instead, Gandalf, Horatio Hornblower or Christopher Columbus. Seventy-one per cent of over-65s know that the famous battle marked every year on 12 July by the Orangemen in Northern Ireland is the Battle of the Boyne. In contrast, this was known by only 18 per cent of 16-24 year-olds. Fifteen per cent of these youngsters thought the Orangemen were celebrating victory at Helms Deep, the fictional battle in Tolkien's *Lord of the Rings*. A survey in 2003[8] revealed that 30 per cent of 11-18 year-olds thought that Oliver Cromwell fought at the Battle of Hastings and a similar number could not name the century for the First World War. Fewer than half of the 200 children questioned knew that Nelson's flagship at Trafalgar was the *Victory*. Similarly, a Channel 4 poll on the history of the monarchy, commissioned to accompany the David Starkey series on the topic, found that only one in ten young people could connect King John to Magna Carta. At the extreme end we read of some youngsters who think Adolf Hitler was Britain's prime minister during World War II and that the Roman occupation happened a mere 150 years ago.[9]

Does any of this matter? Most surely it does. In fact, it matters profoundly—not only for the sake of a good education for our children but also for the future stability and coherence of our multi-racial society. To know the history of one's country is a birthright. It tells us who we are and how we got here. It tells us how our shared values came into being. A people that does not know its history is a people suffering from memory loss, amnesia—a damaging illness. For newcomers to this country, it is equally important. Knowledge of a country's past can be an important means of binding together its people. Without such knowledge a vacuum of ignorance is created, and ignorance and extremism are happy bed fellows. This can have dangerous consequences, as politicians have, belatedly, realised. Consequently, in January 2007 we had the well-intentioned Ajegbo report on 'Diversity and Citizenship',[10] in the wake of the July 7th bombing. It looks for a way forward through citizenship lessons that promote critical thinking about ethnicity, religion and race. Ajegbo argues for history having a central role in a revised citizenship curriculum that teaches British values. His report has been embraced by the Government but, sadly, is unlikely to solve the problem. It fails to address the problem that, in the classroom, 'history' means New History. Indeed, it is because we have New History in the classroom that we have a consequent knowledge vacuum in the first place. In any case, the integrity of history as a subject will be undermined as much by seeing it as a vehicle for delivering 'Britishness' as it has been undermined by seeing it as a vehicle for delivering 'skills' and 'concepts' through its reinvention as New History.

## Selection and manipulation

The New History idea that knowledge of the past should be constructed by pupils for themselves is seductive because it appears to be a way of encouraging independent thinking. The reality, of course, is that the evidence presented to pupils by text books and by teachers has to be carefully selected. In this sense, the process of teaching history has become highly manipulative. Forming opinions about events and personalities on the basis of a scattering of pre-selected and often doctored sources can undermine any balanced understanding. The Schools History Project website provides a host of teaching material that is illustrative of the problem. One unit for its GCSE course is entitled 'Terrorism' and the site provides examples of 'coursework materials' for this unit. Whilst coursework in its present form is to be phased out over the next few years, the material being recommended for current coursework is illustrative of the use to which 'evidence' is being put in the classroom:

> There has hardly been a more obvious topic for this kind of study since the SHP began in 1972 than Terrorism. It fills the news, it startles and frightens, it is interpreted for us by politicians. The current explosion of news and information is overwhelming. Yet the reasons for terrorism, the roots of the violence and a historical perspective are not easy for young people to find. Nor is it easy for teachers wishing to harness their students' interest in the topic to design assessable coursework assignments. On this area of the website you will find various kinds of material intended to help you and your students tackle this topic.[11]

The material being promoted presents terrorism and its victims as having, broadly speaking, equal points of view. After all, 'new history' is about 'value relativism'—all views are equal since history is all a matter of opinion. A pack entitled 'World terrorism since 9/11/01' contains 13 sources. Four of these are about Osama Bin Laden, including one source that provides extracts from his own words across a range of topics and another source that transcribes his words about the September 11th attack. These two pro-Bin Laden sources are 'balanced' only by a fairly neutral biography of Bin Laden and by a copy of the FBI Wanted Poster for him. Across the other nine sources two are pro-US, two are anti-US and four are, broadly, neutral. The final source provides 16 quotations from the world press on the third anniversary of 9/11. Eight of these press reports come from the Islamic world and are largely hostile to the West. The other eight are from Europe and Asia. Five of them are critical of the US. The US press is not represented.

What is clear is that these teaching materials include substantial evidence to justify terrorism. Can one feel that pupils presented with this material are going to be able to come to a balanced historical conclusion? Should such recent topics even be taught as a part of school history lessons? The Schools History Project website also provides teaching material on 'Terrorism and the Middle East', 'The Beslan School siege', 'The kidnapping of Ken Bigley' and 'Press reporting of terrorism'.

## Chronological jumble

When asked about the significance of the 1789 events in France, Zhou En-lie the Chinese Premier (1949-1976) is reported to have said, 'It's too soon to tell'.[12] We may feel that he rather over-stated the case but a sense of perspective across time is, certainly, something that history should provide. Not only is it sorely lacking in the examples quoted from the Schools History Project GCSE syllabus, it has been totally ditched in the History National Curriculum for Key Stages 1 and 2 (ages 5 to 11). Children jump around in time between, for example, Vikings and Victorians, Ancient Greeks and Tudors. They also have to cover a non-European society. This might work well if the teacher were allowed to choose, say, Ancient Egypt for Key Stage 1 (ages 5 to 7) but making it Unit 6 of Key Stage 2 causes chronological confusion for young children who may have just studied 'Britain since 1930'.

The decision to require pupils to study a past non-European society at Key Stage 2 certainly confused the authors of the National Curriculum. As the sole dissenting voice on the group that wrote it, and author of a minority report, I asked those specifically responsible for the non-European unit to which 'Benin' they were referring in their prescribed list of six non-European societies from which teachers have to choose one. They were silent, unaware that there are two Benins. And so, to this day, we have a National

Curriculum that specifies Benin as an area for study but does not indicate which one.

## Landmarks disappear

The History National Curriculum is a distorting mirror. What you think you are seeing is rarely a reality. Take the much trumpeted claim that British history is dominant. Now, for most people, this would mean that pupils have to be taught about the famous personalities and the landmark events such as the battles of Hastings, Bannockburn, Trafalgar or El Alamein. In fact, there is no requirement to teach about any specific personality or battle, not even William the Conqueror and Hastings. However, teachers are provided with some optional examples of what might be taught and these do, indeed, include some landmark events and personalities, like Hastings. However, in the earlier versions of the National Curriculum some of these personalities and events were prescribed. Why, one wonders, are these now only provided as examples? Why are they no longer required to be taught?

Sadly, whilst the original National Curriculum, introduced in 1990, did require the teaching of some landmark events and personalities, it was an unusable document. The assessment system, based on ten levels of attainment across three attainment targets, was all about spurious historical skills and not about knowledge of the content. Dr Anthony Freeman and I were called to 10 Downing Street shortly before the document was due to be published and after it had been agreed by the Secretary of State. Our task was to rescue something from the betrayal of the subject it represented. The Prime Minister, Margaret Thatcher, told me that she was horrified to discover that, amongst other things, a History National Curriculum could leave out the First World War. She ensured that this was added but, at the time, could secure its presence only as an optional topic. To have made it compulsory would have caused the rest of the document to unravel.

With only a few days to go before publication of this New History National Curriculum, all we could do was to make clear the inherent contradiction within it between attainments targets that were about skills and the study units that appeared to be content-based. It was obvious to us that the historical content would simply be a vehicle for teaching the 'skills' and that, as a consequence, the content would be diluted to such an extent that it would be inconsequential. We inserted the word 'knowledge' into the heading of the first Attainment Target so that it read, 'Knowledge and understanding of history'. Since the 25 statements of attainment underneath this heading were, effectively, content-free we were aware that the new curriculum would be unworkable and would have to be revised.

The new Prime Minister, John Major, seemed to understand the arguments. In a letter of 1992 to the General Secretary of the National Union of Teachers he stated:

> So far as history is concerned, the History Curriculum Association and the work of Freeman and McGovern have amply documented challenges to the traditional core of this crucial subject.

The schools minister at the time, Emily Blatch, was determined to act. She had the support of the Secretary of State for Education, John Patten. An *ad hoc* meeting was set up in Eastbourne for the weekend of 15-16 January 1993 to discuss ways forward. It did not involve ministers directly but it was financed by the Government. Following this meeting Emily Blatch was convinced of the need to revise the history curriculum. The Secretary of State agreed but decided that the National Curriculum for all subjects should also be revised.

This great opportunity for restoring a knowledge-based definition of history was lost. The existing curriculum was slimmed down and the new version was given the appearance of having a greater amount of British history within a secure framework of knowledge. This has proved illusory as I said it would when I published my minority report. The Government caved in when Sir Ron (later Lord) Dearing, who had led the entire process of National Curriculum revision, concluded, in his Final Report, that 'even in a subject such as history', the award of a level on the 10-level scale can relate 'to conceptual skills and understanding that are independent of the body of knowledge taught'.[13] He added that history lends itself to the 10-level model because it is 'structured in terms of the mastery of certain skills'.[14] These two statements underpinned the revolution that had taken place—the transformation of history into 'New History'. So-called 'skills', rather than knowledge, now defined the subject. Teach what content you like. It really does not matter. 'New History' is not reliant on any specific content. It is rather like telling children about the concept of a story rather than the story itself.

Of course, none of this was the original intention of the Government, certainly not of the Prime Minister, when the idea of a National Curriculum was born back in the late 1980s. In her memoirs, Margaret Thatcher notes that her educational philosophy 'turned out to be very different from that of those to whom Ken Baker [Secretary of State for Education] entrusted the drawing-up of the national curriculum...'[15] She was fully cognisant of the fact that for the educational establishment 'the national curriculum would be expected to give legitimacy and universal application to the changes which had been made over the last 20 years or so in the content and methods of teaching'.[16] For her, the 'hardest battle' on the National Curriculum was about history. 'Though not an historian myself, I had a very clear—and I had naively imagined uncontroversial—idea of what history was. History is an account of what happened in the past. Learning history, therefore, requires knowledge of events. It is impossible to make sense of such events without absorbing sufficient factual information and without being able to place matters in a clear chronological framework…'[17] She was astute enough to recognise that the proposed membership of the first History Working Group, back in 1989, 'included the author of the definitive work on the New History which, with its emphasis on concepts rather than chronology and empathy rather than facts, was at the root of so much that was going wrong. Ken saw my point and made some changes. But this was only the beginning of the argument.'[18] Subsequent events have proved her right.

In the 1995 revised version of the National Curriculum there was a still a requirement to teach a smattering of landmark events and leaders that have contributed to the evolution of the society we are today—Hastings, Henry VIII, the Glorious Revolution. I had felt that something had been achieved in having these events, at least, mentioned even though I knew that they would be used mainly as a vehicle for teaching 'skills' and 'concepts' through the politically correct perspectives. However, once the hullabaloo died down and the few critics, like myself, had been marginalised, even these 'landmarks' disappeared, quietly removed in 1999 to a list of optional examples of what *might* be taught. There is no longer any requirement at all to teach about any specific personality from the past. Nor is there any requirement to teach about any specific event—other than within a world history context for one unit. The defining landmarks of British history are confined to the optional sections of 'examples' of what might be taught. Back in 1994, in a letter from the architect of the national curriculum, Sir Ron Dearing, schools were told that 'it is very much up to individual schools to determine' whether or not to use the examples. Instead, there is now just a general requirement to include some coverage of the 'development of monarchy' in the unit on medieval Britain, 'crowns, parliaments and people' for the unit on 1500-1750 and the 'expansion of trade and colonisation, industrialisation and political change' for the unit on 1750-1900. The message to history teachers is: 'Pick your own landmarks but make sure you choose ones that will allow you to teach the skills and perspectives.'

The latest proposal for revision, a new history curriculum for Key Stage 3,[19] takes us even further along the path of New History and close to its apotheosis. We now simply have the injunction to teach 'Aspects of British history... from the middle ages to the twentieth century' without reference to any specific event or personality. The 'slave trade' is as close as we get to an event. It is prescribed alongside such concepts as 'political power', 'changing relationships', 'movement and settlement', and 'lives, beliefs, ideas and attitudes'. As for making the 'middle ages' a starting point, one suspects that the authors of this proposal are in a muddle over 'middle'. It should refer to the period between the collapse of the Roman Empire in the West and the beginning of the Renaissance. The new curriculum would need to start 600 years before the Norman Conquest in order to cover this dark ages part of the Middle Ages but there is no indication that coverage of the Saxons and Vikings is intended. Since the existing curriculum has a unit covering the period from 1066 to 1500, one can expect 'middle ages' to be defined by teachers in the same terms.

The new proposals for European and world history also require only 'Aspects' to be taught, with the exception of the two world wars and the holocaust. These continue to be prescribed. Most significant with regard to the proposed coverage of European and world history is the requirement to teach only 'the impact' of 'significant developments and events' rather than events themselves. We are given the example of the 'impact of... the French Revolution and Napoleonic era'—something very different from teaching about the causes and the narrative of the event itself. Doubtless, the 'impact' of events will lend itself more readily to the teaching of the 'life skills' that underpins the new proposals for Key Stage 3. Certainly, the new curriculum makes more overt than ever the unimportance of any specific knowledge and the supreme importance of using history as a vehicle for teaching something else.

Attending the launch of this proposed new secondary curriculum was rather like entering an episode from 'Doctor Who'. The audience was urged to embrace a brave new world of life-skills and to spread the good news to schools. 'Perspectives on the curriculum' called 'lenses' are to determine the new approach. There will be the 'curriculum aims lens', a 'personal development lens' and a 'skills lens'. We were reassured that everything will be in the best interests of the children. In any case, nothing much is, really, going to change. 'Anne Boleyn will still lose her head. Trafalgar will still take place,' joked the QCA's Director of Education in a proclamation that formed a reassuring headline in the *Times Educational Supplement*. But this journal also noted that, for history, 'the chronological approach has been replaced by a thematic one which leaves out specifics'.[20] The reality is that we may continue to see a few old familiar faces in the new proposals but things are not what they seem.

## Multiple perspectives

Constraints on time make the curriculum even more inadequate. The Key Stage 3 (ages 11-14) unit on Britain 1066-1500 is illustrative. The Qualifications and Curriculum Authority's recommended time for this entire unit of 434 years is ten to 15 hours—30 to 43 years per hour—and it has to be taught through a host of politically correct perspectives.

The National Curriculum document states that children must be taught history through four 'diversity' perspectives—'the social, cultural, religious, and ethnic diversity of the societies studied'. In addition, perspectives on 'experiences', on 'ideas', on 'beliefs', and on 'attitudes' relating to each of men, women and children, must be taught—'the experiences and range of ideas, beliefs and attitudes of men, women and children' in the 'periods and societies studied'. This amounts to another 12 perspectives. The focus on perspectives is spelt out explicitly in the statement requiring that history be taught 'from a variety of perspectives including political, religious, social, cultural, aesthetic, economic, technological and scientific'—a further eight perspectives. Although the National Curriculum document does not always use the word 'perspective' there are, in effect, 24 of them. Twenty-six appear in the proposals for a new history curriculum at Key Stage 3.[21] The current National Curriculum document and the proposed changes to Key Stage 3 separate out these perspectives because it requires them to be taught. The obsession with 'political correctness' in most of these perspectives is clear. Take any landmark personality or event in history and start applying these perspectives to its teaching and we see how the familiar and the famous can easily become the unfamiliar and the uninformative.

As if these 24 perspectives were not enough, children must also be taught 'aspects of the histories of England, Ireland, Scotland and Wales where appropriate'. Add to this the over-riding requirement to teach a range of so-called skills relating to 'historical interpretation' and 'historical enquiry' and one is left asking precisely how much time will be spent on, say, the Battle of Agincourt, when there is not even a requirement to teach a military perspective on any aspect of history in the National Curriculum.

These perspectives act as a kind of filter. If a battle is taught it is as likely to be through a 'social' or 'gender' perspective—conditions on board HMS Victory or the role of women in World War II munitions factories—than it is to be about military events at Trafalgar or El Alamein. When children learn about Elizabeth I they are as likely to learn about how she dressed and went about her daily life as they are about what she did. The unfolding narrative of what happened across the Tudor period does not have to be covered. Edward VI and Mary I do not even get a specific mention in the examples of what might be covered under the Tudors.

In 1999 the Government decided that, as from September 2000, specified personalities and events would be removed from the history curriculum altogether. How did history teachers react? On its website the Historical Association calls itself 'the voice for History ...committed to the encouragement and support of history teaching at all levels of education'. It is, certainly, a mouthpiece for history teachers and publishes journals for both primary and for secondary school teachers. Sean Lang, its honorary secretary, was quoted in the *Times Educational Supplement* as stating:

> The curriculum in practice is already much more flexible than it seems on paper. Teachers have already slimmed it down. Every child gets taught the Tudors and the two world wars but is unlikely to study the Stuarts and post-war Britain although they are all statutory. I would advise people not to be alarmed by the slimming down of content. It only reflects what happens on the ground.[22]

In other words—history has become the property of the teachers. They can do what they want with it. So goodbye and good riddance to the Stuarts!

By January 2007 the same honorary secretary of the HA seemed to have changed his position. He was now lamenting the fact that 'we have huge gaps in our historical coverage. Schools seem to have neglected most of the seventeenth and eighteenth centuries. They tend to leap straight from the Tudors to the Victorians, missing out a lot on the way.'[23] He added that this 'is a great shame',[24] without ever recognising that the cause of this state of affairs is the teaching demands of New History, which his association had promoted so vigorously.

As 'would be' custodians of school history teaching and the national memory, the Historical Association has let us down. It has been openly antipathetic to teaching the landmarks of British history and has promoted New History with zeal. If history teachers are choosing to teach only parts of the National Curriculum we can be fairly sure that it will be short on content and heavy on 'skills' and the politically correct perspectives. When, in March 2000, the Government announced its wish to see an element of British history in all GCSE history courses, the response from the Historical Association was as depressing as it was predictable. Ben Walsh, chairman of the Association's secondary committee, told the *Times Educational Supplement*:

> We are utterly dismayed by this proposal. We oppose it both as a point of principle and because it will bring problems for schools — in terms of new books and reorganisation. Nobody in the mainstream history community has asked for this or believes it is a good idea.[25]

## Peterloo not Waterloo

A survey of history teachers commissioned by the Qualifications and Curriculum Authority in 1999 showed that an overwhelming majority was against the inclusion of a traditional and mainly political British history course for

GCSE. These courses have now disappeared and the political history of Britain only gets a look in alongside modern social and economic history. GCSE pupils can study such topics as 'Race relations in a multi-cultural society since 1945' or 'The impact of cinema, radio and television since 1918', but landmark events such as the Norman Conquest, the Reformation or the Glorious Revolution have been cast into examination oblivion at GCSE.

If there is any doubt about where we are being led by the New History, one need only look at the school history text books it has spawned to support the National Curriculum. *Minds and Machines: Britain 1750-1900* is illustrative. It is not some fringe publishing venture by trendy educational zealots but part of a major publishing venture by Longman, that most respectable and mainstream of educational publishers. It consists of four text books covering the period from 1066 to the end of the twentieth century and claims to 'ensure thorough coverage of the National Curriculum'.

This is how Longman promotes the series on its website:

## Welcome to Think Through History
The famous enquiry-based approach that's still second-to-none

*Think Through History*, an exciting enquiry-based approach built around key historical issues and characters, has met with great success in schools. The series comprises four Students' Books, each tailor-made for an area of the revised curriculum. Each Student's Book is accompanied by a Teacher's Book containing 60 differentiated copymasters with a wide range of activities for all abilities.

One of two editors of the series, and co-author of *Minds and Machines: Britain 1750-1900*, is a senior lecturer in the Education Faculty at the University of Cambridge, a leading member of the Historical Association and editor of its journal *Teaching History*.

Traditional heroes including Clive of India, General Wolfe, Admiral Nelson, Florence Nightingale and General Gordon are all excluded from this National Curriculum text book on the period from 1750 to 1900. The Duke of Wellington's role in history is confined to his opposition to the Chartists. There is no mention of his role at Waterloo: the book promotes Peterloo, not Waterloo. Nor do many prime ministers get much of a look in. Pitt the Elder, Pitt the Younger and Peel are all sidelined. Palmerston and Gladstone get minor walk-on roles. Instead, new 'heroes' appear, including the American Chief Crowfoot, the African Chief Lobengula, the Fijian Chief Cakobau, the Indian Princess Rani Lakshmi, an Aborigine teacher named Bessy Cameron and Josephine Butler, a British campaigner against sexually transmitted diseases.

Landmark events and topics such as the Seven Years' War, the American Revolution, the Napoleonic Wars, the Crimean War and the Irish Question are among major topics which are either dismissed in a few sentences or totally ignored. Instead, children are provided with a feminist study of Victorian prostitution, sex and sexually transmitted diseases. Pupils are informed that '...the law treated women's bodies as pieces of meat'. And, in order to provide appropriate evidence for empathising with 'the rulers and the ruled' of the British Empire the authors of the book write: '...we have tried to imagine what they would tell us if they were to come back from the dead'. We thus learn that an undead Princess Rani Lakshmi would feel the need to tell us: 'The British punished survivors by firing canon balls through them at point blank range.' A resurrected Chief Lobengula would apparently say: 'My men bravely stood up to the British who cut them down with their canons and machine guns. Soon afterwards I died. My people were conquered and our lands taken.' Cecil Rhodes's message to us from beyond the grave rather confirms what a bad lot we

Brits are. He is made to say: 'I made a fortune... But that was not enough for me: I wanted to change history. We British were the best people in the world so I wanted to control as much of the world as possible.'

The book is more concerned with leading immature youngsters towards superficial moral judgements than it is in providing them with knowledge. Many of the chapter headings are dominated by gloom, doom and despair, suffering and desperation, injustice and exploitation: 'White Gold & Black Misery', 'Fingers weary and worn', 'A perfect wilderness of foulness', 'Pauper places', 'Riot and Reform', 'A policy of sewage'. It is in these terms that the authors have interpreted the National Curriculum and the National Curriculum encourages such a 'free for all' in the choice of content. It accommodates just about anything. However, there is no such latitude with the prescribed 'skills', 'concepts' and perspectives. These are nailed down and have to be taught.

*Minds and Machines: Britain 1750-1900*, then, fits perfectly with the New History National Curriculum, just as Longman claims. Furthermore, in terms of educational respectability and credibility, its authors are from the 'top drawer'. According to the publishers, the book has 'met with great success in schools'. Doubtless it has been seen in action countless times by Ofsted inspectors. And, as the Historical Association is fond of pointing out, Ofsted rate history as one of the best taught subjects. Certainly, if one evaluates history teaching in terms of the extent to which it is faithful to the National Curriculum's New History, I am sure that the inspectors are right. The pupils are getting what they are supposed to be getting. Even the voice of the 'undead' can count as a valid pathway to understanding and truth. The examples quoted represent the reality of National Curriculum History. The punters, of course, have spotted the fake. Too often, New History fails to engage their interest. In February 2007 it was reported by Ofsted's history adviser that seven out of ten pupils drop the subject at the earliest opportunity, aged fourteen.[26] The subject now accounts for only four per cent of the total number of papers sat by GCSE candidates.[27] Given that the GCSE version of the subject is considerably less demanding than the GCE 'O' level exam, still being sat by candidates overseas,[28] one can hardly explain away the unpopularity of the subject in terms of it being too academically challenging. Indeed, recent research at the Institute of Education has indicated that large numbers of 13 and 14 year-olds in comprehensive schools want their lessons to be harder.[29] As far as history is concerned the educational junk diet of New History is, quite simply, a 'turn-off'. In percentage terms, 14+ history is now much less popular than it was when GCE 'O' level was also available, not only abroad, but also in this country. Whilst children vote with their feet, too many history teachers are in denial of the problem and have their heads buried in the sand.

## Separating history from New History

This revolution has gone largely, but not completely, unnoticed by parliament. In 2000, for example, Baroness Blatch made a speech to the House of Lords in which she recalled a visit, as Schools Minister, to a school history lesson:

> ...I visited a school, which will have to remain nameless, where I was told that they taught all subjects through prejudice, racism, gender and conflict. Apart from needing to be held down by my officials when I heard that, what went through my mind was the denial of the glories of literature and history to those pupils. This is not to say that prejudice, racism, gender and conflict are not important in themselves, but to teach all subjects through those themes seemed to be almost a criminal activity on the children. But there seems to be a return to that.[30]

Occasionally, also, we hear the voice of an eminent historian raising questions about what is going on in the name of history. Most recently, David Starkey has raised a banner of dissent by questioning the narrow focus of current A-level syllabuses and the obsession with pupils having to construct the past for themselves through the massively time-consuming evaluation of evidence. The Historical Association jumped in, immediately, to marginalise Starkey. Heather Scott, the current chairman of its secondary committee, trotted out the usual denial: 'Ofsted has said that history is the best taught subject at schools. It is fantastic... I think that he is out of touch with current teaching.' [31]

The problem for Starkey and others like him, even the Prince of Wales, is that they simply do not have the detailed knowledge and understanding of what has been going on in the name of history over the past 40 years. Their instincts tell them that something is wrong but they know too little to really engage in debate with the 'experts' from the world of education. Fundamentally, they have not fully grasped that school history and school New History have little in common and should, probably, be taught separately.

Traditionally, the central concern of school history has been knowledge of the past, presented as an unfolding narrative. These days it seems necessary to defend knowledge and to stress it does not equate with rote learning. On the contrary it is knowledge that humanises us. We cannot think independently without it. The more we know, the more we understand. Knowledge, in the form of 'content', therefore, is at the heart of traditional school history.

In contrast, New History is not centrally concerned with 'content'. 'Content' is simply a vehicle for teaching 'skills', 'concepts' and 'perspectives'. Children have to be taught to construct the past for themselves using evidence—sometimes carefully selected, sometimes randomly selected, usually 'doctored' and always insufficient to do the job properly. This is a very time-consuming process and the better it is done, the longer it takes. If you teach New History there will not be enough time to teach an unfolding narrative—hence the Historical Association's recognition that the Stuarts have been ditched.

Starkey's criticism of current A-level syllabuses in history for being too narrow is, in a sense, misplaced if seen against the logic of the New History. His concern that pupils study only a half of the reign of Henry VIII or that they study Hitler without covering World War II, matters not a jot in the context of the redefined subject. The whole point of the New History is that any content will do. Content is just the ass that has to carry the sociological baggage of 'skills', 'concepts' and 'perspectives'. The exam boards claim that the new range of AS/A-level syllabuses to be examined from 2007 will offer greater breadth but pupils will still have the opportunity to choose such narrowly focused topics as 'The King's Faithful Servant? The Age of Wolsey, 1509-29'. For broader units such as 'Life in Authoritarian Regimes: Nazi Germany and Soviet Russia in the 1930s' schools will be able to choose to teach the whole unit or just half of it. The syllabuses also have the usual New History obsession with 'skills', 'concepts' and 'perspectives'—Byzantine in their complexity. Teachers have to be provided with 'Key skills mapping' to guide them through the labyrinth.[32]

Recently, there has been some Government recognition that aspects of educational dogma have been damaging to our children. The dogma that confined phonics to the periphery in the teaching of reading has, finally, been over-turned. The new primary framework published by the DfES in October 2006 raises expectations in mathematics. Not so long ago these changes would have been unthinkable. Now, we need to review our expectations for history. 'The experts know best', is what we have been led to believe. But what

Churchill said of science applies equally to 'experts'—they should be on tap, not on top.

So where do we go from here? Just as candidates for English and English Literature GCSE can now, apparently, gain A* without reading a book,[33] so pupils can achieve high marks in history without actually knowing very much about the past. If, as the Historical Association claims, it is OK to ditch the Stuarts, then it is OK to ditch anything. Content is really not very important for the New History.

The way forward for history is to separate it from 'New History' altogether, in order to allow it to be taught as an unfolding narrative. This will involve lots of story-telling and story reading—something loved by both children and adults. It would not exclude looking at evidence, where this enhances the story. A visit to the Tower of London, for example, would enhance many a tale of the past.

'Story-telling' should become a formal part of teacher training and LEAs should consider employing story-tellers for schools to share. Television and radio should consider a children's equivalent of such programmes as Simon's Schama's *History of Britain,* David Starkey's *Monarchy* and Mark Hedgecoe's *Ancient Rome.* A new generation of story-books needs to be published to highlight the excitement of the past and its landmarks for this country and for other countries. If this leads to a bias towards pride in our own national identity, so be it. What a welcome 'failing' in these fragmented times that would be. It would, certainly, be far better than the current practice of selecting, doctoring and even inventing 'evidence' in the name of so-called historical 'skills'. Currently, the custodians of our national identity are the Blue Badge guides and the Beefeaters. They spend much of their time with foreign tourists. But, surely, the story of our national past is the birthright of children in this country.

If 'New History' is to continue, its source material should be tailor-made and fictional since this allows it to be taught more effectively. Already, New History text books are moving in this direction. A New History study of 'The Hobbit' or of 'Lord of the Rings' would enhance this trend. Indeed, I have had teachers writing to me to suggest that the best way to teach about the Vikings attacks on Britain is to invent diaries for them. Since the Vikings at that time were, largely, illiterate these invented diaries can be used to offset the accounts written by the literate Anglo-Saxons. This approach, whilst less imaginative than using the 'undead', is another sword in the armoury of New History as it fights the battle for 'skills', 'concepts' and 'perspectives'.

Of course, school history centred on narrative does not mean that we should not cover the 'shameful' bits of our own past or, indeed, the past of other countries. Whether one is looking at Ethelred II 'Unraed', or at Neville Chamberlain, children need to understand the futility of appeasement through the stories of it. They also need to know the story of how the British enslaved conquered peoples and of how, once upon a time, the inhabitants of this island were enslaved, too; not least by an African Emperor who died in Eboracum (York). The government-inspired QCA proposal for slavery within the British Empire to be a compulsory part of a the new history curriculum at Key Stage 3 fails to address the fact of slavery being a shared experience across the whole of time and across the entire globe—present as well as past. Telling only a part of the story will breed misunderstanding. By all means, let us also tell the horror stories such as the potato famine in Ireland but let us not forget that some of those who fled the famine became the exterminators of the native populations of north America. Through their encounters with stories, children will learn what people are like. They will learn that people act bravely or savagely, not because they are British or German or Indian or Nigerian, but because they are people and that is what people do.

The New History has failed adequately to provide our children with the one thing that distinguishes history from all other subjects in the curriculum—knowledge of the past. It is time to restore the unfolding narrative of the past and through it to weave some magic back into our teaching methodology.

# Appendix 1
# Perspectives through which history has to be taught according to the National Curriculum

1   The experiences of men
2   The experiences of women
3   The experiences of children
4   The range of ideas of men
5   The range of ideas of women
6   The range of ideas of children
7   The beliefs of men
8   The beliefs of women
9   The beliefs of children
10  The attitudes of men
11  The attitudes of women
12  The attitudes of children
13  The social diversity of the societies studied both in Britain and the wider world
14  The cultural diversity of the societies studied both in Britain and the wider world
15  The religious diversity of the societies studied both in Britain and the wider world
16  The ethnic diversity of the societies studied both in Britain and the wider world
17  Political
18  Religious
19  Social
20  Cultural
21  Aesthetic
22  Economic
23  Technological
24  Scientific

**The statutory requirement to teach perspectives 1-24
are set in the National Curriculum as follows:**
*Pupils should be taught:*

*a. of the periods and societies studied including the experiences and range of ideas, beliefs and attitudes of men, women and children in the past*

*b. to describe and analyse the relationships between the characteristic features about the social, cultural, religious and ethnic diversity of the societies studied, both in Britain and the wider world*

*In their study of local, British, European and world history, pupils should be taught about:*

*b. history from a variety of perspectives including political, religious, social, cultural, aesthetic, economic, technological and scientific*

# Appendix 2
## Perspectives through which history will have to be taught according to the QCA proposals for a revised History National Curriculum commencing in 2008

1   The diverse experiences of men in the context of cultural, ethnic and religious diversity
2   The diverse experiences of women in the context of cultural, ethnic and religious diversity
3   The diverse experiences of children in the context of cultural, ethnic and religious diversity
4   The range of ideas of men in the context of cultural, ethnic and religious diversity
5   The range of ideas of women in the context of cultural, ethnic and   religious diversity
6   The range of ideas of children in the context of cultural, ethnic and religious diversity
7   The beliefs of men in the context of cultural, ethnic and religious diversity
8   The beliefs of women in the context of cultural, ethnic and religious diversity
9   The beliefs of children in the context of cultural, ethnic and religious diversity
10   The attitudes of men in the context of cultural, ethnic and religious diversity
11   The attitudes of women in the context of cultural, ethnic and religious diversity
12   The attitudes of children in the context of cultural, ethnic and religious diversity
13   Values
14   Racial equality
15   Regional diversity
16   Linguistic diversity
17   Political
18   Religious
19   Social
20   Cultural
21   Aesthetic
22   Economic
23   Technological
24   Scientific
25   Arts
26   Ideas

The proposals for a revised Key Stage 3 National Curriculum
for history sets out perspectives 1-26 as follows:

Cultural, ethnic and religious diversity

Understanding the diverse experiences and the range of ideas, beliefs and attitudes of men, women and children in past societies and how these have shaped the world.

Pupils should learn about cultural, ethnic and religious diversity and racial equality. Diversity exists between groups due to cultural, ethnic, regional, linguistic, social, economic, technological, political and religious differences and exists within groups between individuals.

Explore the ways in which the past has helped shape identities, shared cultures, values and attitudes today.

Examine history from a variety of perspectives, including political, religious, social, cultural, aesthetic, economic, technological and scientific.

This includes exploring past societies through their arts, sciences, technologies, beliefs and ideas and to see how these have affected and been affected by historical change.

# Foreign Languages Without Tears?

# Shirley Lawes

## *The present context and the recent past*

In recent times attitudes to knowledge in the broader sense have become more functional and the aims and purposes of education have become closely linked to the perceived needs of society and the economy rather than that of the intellectual development of the individual. The over-emphasis on outcomes, the idea that we should be able to *measure* at the end of each lesson what pupils have learned, is a fundamental shift in how we understand knowledge. No longer do we see any intrinsic value in education; 'useful' knowledge is all that counts. From this perspective, the study of foreign languages becomes a marginal pursuit. When education is presented to young people as being of only instrumental value in getting a job, or worse, raising their self-esteem, it is reduced to a set of 'skills' that eschews the opening of minds and developing the intellect.

In this climate, the place of foreign languages in the school curriculum, and their value in relation to other subjects, has become more vulnerable to intervention by government. Moreover, the decline in interest over a number of years, in England at least, in languages as an area of academic study at undergraduate level during a period when foreign languages were compulsory in the school curriculum up to the age of 16, has increased this vulnerability. Mastery of a foreign language is a lifetime pursuit that doesn't fit well into the current pre-packaged view of knowledge. We can criticise the low levels of 'communicative competence' achieved by learners in secondary schools, blame it on negative attitudes of pupils in an anglophone world, poor teaching or ineffective

86

methodology—some of which may be true, some of the time. However, the real problem is a much deeper one.

The National Languages Strategy introduced quite sweeping changes regarding when and how foreign languages should be taught in schools and has also impacted on which languages feature on the school curriculum. Despite the rhetoric and exhortation of policy-makers and government advisors, the teaching and learning of modern languages is being pushed to the margins of education at all levels. The promotion of foreign language learning in primary education will do nothing to remedy the situation because it can never be more than a marginal activity in this sector, partly because it is only an *entitlement*. Nevertheless, this initiative is the linchpin of current government policy. The Key Stage 3 Framework within the National Languages Strategy represents a quite radical shift in government policy which has been hailed as an attempt to indicate a firm political commitment to foreign language learning and a recognition of the importance of increasing Britain's foreign language capacity in both economic and educational terms, while at the same time acknowledging the difficulty of the subject area. Perhaps somewhat cynically, it might be seen as a misguided attempt to demonstrate a commitment to boost a somewhat beleaguered curriculum area that will have long-term deleterious effects on foreign languages in this country.

It is now two years since the government decided that pupils should be allowed to choose to continue learning a foreign language at Key Stage 4, and the picture is bleak. Even the minority of state schools that still insist on keeping modern languages compulsory are under pressure to take a more relaxed view with some pupils and, as a result, some young people are only getting one or two years' teaching before they are actually required to give up. In over 70 per cent of state schools the study of a foreign language is no longer compulsory after Year 9 and some schools are even taking languages off the curriculum after six months for 'less able' pupils.[1] The knock-on effect on universities in the next few years will be devastating. Already, 30 per cent of all new young modern languages undergraduates now come from the independent sector where the study of languages continues to be compulsory to GCSE level. Foreign languages are once again becoming an elitist subject area.

When the UK became a member of the European Economic Community in 1973, many teachers of foreign languages imagined the dawn of a new era for their subject discipline in schools. Although by that time the majority of 11-year-olds were learning a foreign language, usually French, in secondary school, the subject area was still seen by many as academic and elitist. Membership of the EEC raised awareness and concerns outside the education community about the UK's poor overall language capability and fears were expressed that opportunities would be missed to reap the full benefit of EEC membership. In 1976 Prime Minister James Callaghan launched 'The Great Debate' on education in a landmark speech at Ruskin College, Oxford, in which he identified 'the need to improve relations between industry and education'.[2] The idea that foreign language learning might have a practical use for more than a very tiny portion of the population was a challenge that raised issues of what should be learned and how. Importantly, the Ruskin College speech indicated for the first time that education should be linked to the needs of the economy and that educational decisions should not be left only to educators: government and other interested parties had a role to play in educational decision-making.

The combination of membership of the EEC and the shift in the relationship between education and society had an impact on the teaching and learning of foreign languages. Firstly, for foreign language teachers, membership of the

EEC signalled a possible change in attitudes towards language learning. Greater numbers and a wider range of learner ability, together with the new opportunities for job mobility in the EEC that many people envisaged, led many teachers to believe that learners might see foreign languages as more attractive and relevant if they had a vocational purpose. The perceived value and purpose of foreign languages began to change quite rapidly. Developments in teaching methodology were aimed at promoting foreign languages for communication, 'authenticity' of task and materials, and the use of native speakers modelling everyday language. The aim was to make foreign languages more accessible to a wider range of pupils and to make their study more relevant. As well-intentioned as these initiatives were, the emphasis on the functional use of language in practical situations paved the way for an emptying out of any serious linguistic or cultural content in favour of what was to become little more than a survival toolkit for a holiday abroad.

A key milestone in the history of foreign languages is the Education Reform Act of 1988 and the subsequent introduction of the National Curriculum for Schools in 1991. Indeed this was a watershed in education in England and Wales. Increased intervention by government in education continued throughout the 1990s up to the present time, to the point where all aspects of schooling and school life, from school meals to classroom discipline, are now the subject of policy initiatives that prescribe practice. This is no less true of the foreign languages curriculum area. Education generally, and foreign languages specifically, are now seen as important objects of political interest and public policy, in which the government is involved to a far greater extent than at any time in the past. For example, the imposition of 'cross-curricular themes' such as ICT, the environment and citizenship education as well as the requirement for all teachers to be concerned with literacy and numeracy skills, represents an erosion of our understanding of the subject discipline of foreign languages, and reflects a change in how we understand subject knowledge.

Responses to recent changes in foreign language curriculum provision range from applause, tinged with nervousness about how realistic the policies are,[3] to dismay from those who fear for the future of foreign languages at all levels now that they have been made optional on the school curriculum from the age of 14. Whether seen as a further watershed, or a crisis, it is clear that the changes have fuelled both concern and debate over what the subject area should constitute, who it should be for and why it is important. It is now more difficult to justify foreign languages as a subject discipline on its own terms, at a time when what should be taught in schools is increasingly called into question.

The recent Languages Review conducted by Lord Dearing confirmed his support of government policy by placing great emphasis on the importance of foreign language learning in the primary school and also recommended numerous ways of reinvigorating foreign languages in the secondary school curriculum. However, he side-stepped the most contentious issue and failed to call for a reversal of policy on the optional status of foreign languages at Key Stage 4, preferring to recommend 'incentives' to schools to encourage greater participation.

Where Dearing took an ambivalent stand on optionality,[4] others have been more forthright in expressing their views. Kevin Williams, for example, maintains that any compulsory status of foreign languages in the secondary school curriculum is misguided, arguing his case at a time when a 'languages for all' policy throughout the secondary curriculum applied. Firstly, he maintains, correctly, that there are 'serious defects in the argument for teaching modern foreign languages on grounds of their vocational usefulness or their role in the generation of wealth'.[5] Secondly he considers that cultural and 'civic' arguments are equally ineffective. However, he confirms that all young people should be 'entitled to the opportunity' of learning at least one foreign language, but that this should be for only one year after which they should be allowed to give up on the grounds that they should not be made to learn something that they are not interested in or have no aptitude for. There are many counter-arguments to this, but Williams is used here as an example of the thinking in some quarters that has clearly now gained considerable ground, given the optional status; that is, that many young people are not capable of learning foreign languages beyond a very basic level. Although the sentiment is often not expressed in such overt terms, or even argued as cogently as Williams does, it is now central to current policy. One justification for removing the compulsion to learn foreign languages up to GCSE level is that many young people do not *like* foreign languages and that they should be given the opportunity to give them up at the end of Key Stage 3 in order to learn something more useful and relevant to them. The underlying message here is that most young people in England are not intellectually capable of foreign language learning, and that foreign languages are not really that important. However, messages from government are contradictory, confusing and contemptuous of young people. The recently published review of the National Curriculum suggests that schools should be offering Chinese, Arabic and Japanese instead of the traditional European languages. How does this relate to the idea that languages are too hard for many young people? The implicit message is that only some young people should be offered such opportunities.

## How foreign languages are currently promoted

But what is it that we might want young people to aspire to? If the ultimate goal and perhaps abilities of most foreign language learners falls far short of 'mastery' or even 'communicative competence' in its real sense, should more realistic 'benchmarks' be applied? Or could it be that, by rejecting the possibility of the highest possible level of achievement, learners restrict their aspirations and have lower horizons, that teachers lower their expectations of their pupils and that potential is lost or not achieved? At what point does a foreign language become an operational skill? These are questions that we might ask in relation to how the life-long occupation of learning a foreign language is marked out in stages and how decisions are made about who should learn what.

The view of policy makers of the place and value of foreign language learning in our education system is that it is a functional skill with an assumed practical purpose relevant to business needs or future employment. This functionalism is enlivened by trying to make foreign languages relevant and entertaining by relating them entirely to the lives of pupils themselves or young people in other countries; by spending time on learning to talk about topical issues such as healthy eating and the environment in simplistic terms such as '*les pommes sont bonnes, les frites ne sont pas bonnes*' ('apples are good', 'chips are bad') that is entirely unimaginative but certainly conveys a moral message. In a desperate attempt to make foreign languages more appealing, Spanish is currently being promoted over other languages because more pupils are likely to use it on holiday. As was noted above, Arabic, Chinese and Japanese are suddenly in fashion, where once Russian was seen as the language of the future. In fact, *what* language is taught is actually less important than *why* it is being taught.

These are impoverished views of foreign language learning that indicate nothing about what a foreign language could give young people. They reduce foreign language study to a functional skill that teaches the sort of thing you find in a 'get by' phrase book. It is selling young people short and is unlikely to inspire anyone to see languages as anything other than mechanical and boring. Moreover, to resurrect old vocational arguments for foreign language learning is patronising and false. Young people were never fooled by the idea that 'you'll get a better job if you speak a language' and they are unlikely to be now, given the dominance of English as a world language. While it is true that there are now more opportunities than there used to be for using languages at the workplace, the level of competence needed is far beyond GCSE and even A-level. The study of foreign languages has the potential of favouring the universal over the particular in a unique way, of providing a window on the world by enriching people's lives and opening them up to other cultures and literatures, and this could be achieved right from the early stages of foreign language learning if more teachers were confident enough to look beyond the next test and take the long view.

## *Defending foreign languages as a subject discipline*

The preoccupation with what is 'relevant' to young people, with what relates to their limited experience of the world in an instrumental sense, has prevented us from seeking to broaden their horizons and provide cultural insights in a special way that can leave a lasting impression on them. It is often suggested that the study of literature is not relevant to young people. This is patronising and reveals a low opinion of what they are capable of. Young people today are no less capable of studying literature, and no less likely to be inspired by it, than they were in the past. By exposing young people to the best that humanity has achieved and aspired to, the best that is known and thought, we are perhaps assigning a higher purpose to education. What we are doing is taking areas of knowledge that have traditionally been the preserve of a tiny section of society and reclaiming them for everyone. By introducing young people to the culture of a foreign country through the greatest and most creative works that a society or an individual has achieved, we can encourage them to see that there is more to the foreign language and culture than the functional and sometimes banal representations they normally experience. In this way, learners of foreign languages move beyond their parochial, subjective experiences, to appreciate cultural achievements that have spread beyond national boundaries and are part of universal *human* culture. This is the liberating potential of foreign languages that teachers can harness to inspire their learners. Have we lost the ability to inspire young people? We have, if we really believe that everything must be made relevant to their experience and their limited view of the world.

Defences of foreign languages as a field of knowledge in its own terms are few and far between at the present time. Even those who recognise the contribution of foreign languages to an all-round education and personal develop-ment of individuals, and the subject's potential for broadening the horizons of young people, often still feel the need to justify their arguments in instrumental and functional terms. What such arguments miss is what is unique about foreign languages. Foreign language study has a unique transformational capacity that differentiates it from other subject disciplines in the potential that knowledge of foreign languages has of opening individuals up to human culture and to 'emancipate the learner from parochialism'.[6] Foreign languages have the unique potential of breaking down barriers between people and countries and promoting a sense of universalism in an individualised world.[7] This is at the heart of what makes the study of foreign languages unique.

There are at least two myths about foreign languages that are popularly held views today. Firstly that the British are 'no good at learning languages'; and, secondly, that foreign languages are not popular because English is the dominant world language. These are merely excuses for failure both in terms of the individual and of foreign languages as a subject discipline. While one would not deny that many people *think* they are not good at foreign languages, there is no evidence to suggest that this is an inherent feature of the British character or that there is some genetic peculiarity about the British, or indeed that not everyone is capable of learning a foreign language.

Two examples of recent research point to some of the more plausible explanations for the negativity that surrounds foreign languages at the present time. A recent study by Milton and Meara[8] compares foreign language learning experience and performance of 14-year-old British, Greek and German pupils. Their findings did indeed identify significantly poorer foreign language performance amongst the British students as compared with their European counterparts, but that this was largely attributed to the fact they spent significantly less time in foreign language learning. The study showed that English students were set lower goals and it suggested that learning needs were not being met either in terms of offering sufficient challenge for the most able or the necessary support for the less able in comparison with those abroad. It also raised issues of methodology as a possible contributing factor. Graham,[9] in a study of pupils' learning strategies in Years 11, 12 and 13, found that learners themselves attributed their lack of success to their own lack of ability, despite the fact that they were 'successful' learners. Graham's research found that success or failure were related to how students went about tasks and that students can be helped to adopt a more positive approach to success and failure by training them to attribute their success to the learning strategies they use. Equally, they can be helped to improve their learning strategies in a systematic way by the teacher. Interest in learning strategies is gaining ground and there is a growing body of research and evidence from practice to suggest that it is an area that can contribute significantly to improving learners' performance in foreign languages and thereby dispelling the myth that the British are poor at languages.

There is some substance to the argument that the dominant role of English as a world language has had a detrimental effect on foreign language learning. Indeed, the Milton and Meara study referred to above confirmed that learners of English in Greece and Germany have a high instrumental motivation to learn, which contributed to their higher achievement in foreign languages. They concluded that this is not the same for English pupils learning a foreign language. However, instrumental arguments for learning are problematic in and of themselves, because they are restrictive and reductive. But instrumental and functional arguments are prevalent and difficult to challenge in the present climate where foreign languages are valued largely for their functional use. On the other hand, if we take the view that foreign languages have a broader cultural and intellectual role to play both in education and society, as well as contributing to the personal enrichment of the individual, then the position of the English language takes on a relative rather than dominant position.

Where does the teacher of foreign languages stand in all this? A belief in the value of foreign languages as a subject discipline, a passion for their subject, and a belief in their ability to inspire young people to share their passion are pre-requisites for successful teaching and indispensable to the future of foreign language learning at all levels. Whatever new structures or curriculum initiatives may be introduced by policy-makers, it is still teachers who have the expert subject knowledge and it is their belief in and passion for their subject that enables them to inspire learners. In a real sense, knowledge is power. Expert subject knowledge is the basis of a teacher's professional expertise. Belief in the value of foreign languages as a subject discipline is therefore paramount, and of overriding importance to whatever policies might be imposed from without. The sad thing is that it is linguists, the foreign language educators, who have themselves capitulated to the reductionist view of foreign language learning in a desperate attempt to preserve and promote foreign languages. But if we ask ourselves the question, what is most likely to *inspire* young people, awaken their curiosity for foreign language learning, develop their cognitive abilities and creativity, is it going to be functional communication or could it be something more? It is easier, perhaps, to challenge instrumental attitudes to knowledge in young people, than in policy-makers and professionals and in society at large. Knowledge of other languages will always be of importance as a cultural achievement whether or not it is economically important as English becomes the global language of business. Unless teachers make this educational argument and abandon functional and vocational defences of their subject, foreign language learning will go into terminal decline in British schools.

# Teaching By Numbers

## Simon Patterson

Having taught philosophy and other subjects at degree level for almost 30 years, I decided to take early retirement with a view to training to become a maths teacher. I had studied mathematics to degree level, but many years ago and as part of a broader programme of study, and so I took advantage of a two year 0.5 contract to embark upon an Open University degree course in mathematics. I was close to completing this course when I was accepted onto the Graduate Teacher Programme and started my employment (in September 2001) as an untrained teacher of mathematics, to be trained by the school employing me, with the expectation that I would become a newly qualified teacher (NQT) by the end of the year and, if I succeeded in obtaining a further year's employment, a fully qualified teacher, after a second year of training. In the event I was forced to resign by a temporarily disabling illness, there being no way to reschedule a training programme linked to a one-year contract of employment. At the time, I was enormously disappointed. In retrospect, I doubt if I would ever have derived satisfaction from teaching mathematics the way it seems that it must now be taught in schools.

There are many reasons for this: the culture of constant appraisal, the disempowerment of the classroom teacher, the time devoted to responding to ministerial directives, the obsessive concern about grades, the replacement of a two-year A-level syllabus by shorter modules assessed at the end of each half-year. However, a principal reason stems from some of the unintended effects on teaching, in Key Stages 1 to 4, of the National Curriculum in mathematics.

## *What to teach and how to teach it*

The National Curriculum in mathematics (NCM) employs 'attainment targets' and 'level descriptions' to set out the 'knowledge, skills and understanding that pupils of different abilities and maturities are expected to have at the end of each Key Stage'[1] and the 'Framework for teaching mathematics' provides detailed objectives for planning and teaching mathematics for pupils aged five to 11.[2] One can think of the 'attainment targets' as specifying the syllabus which all students must follow through Key Stages 1 to 3, and as providing a choice between two programmes of study (a *foundation* and *higher*) at Key Stage 4. The 'level descriptions' provide a basis for making judgements about pupils' performance at the end of each Key Stage, and determining which programme of study is appropriate at Key Stage 4.

Attainment targets are specified under different headings, as follows:

| Key Stage 1 (5-7 yrs, Yr groups 1-2) | | Key Stage 2 (9-11 yrs, Yr groups 3-6) | |
|---|---|---|---|
| Ma2 | Number | Ma2 | Number |
| Ma3 | Shape, space and measures | Ma3 | Shape, space and measures |
| | | Ma4 | Handling data |
| Key Stage 3 (11-14 yrs, Yr groups 7-9) | | Key Stage 4 (14-16 yrs, Yr groups 10-11) | |
| Ma2 | Number and algebra | Ma2 | Number and algebra |
| Ma3 | Shape, space and measures | Ma3 | Shape, space and measures |
| Ma4 | Handling data | Ma4 | Handling data |

[A marginal note (NCM, p. 16) explains that there is no programme of study corresponding to Ma1 (using and applying mathematics) since the teaching 'requirements relating to this attainment target are included within the other sections of the programme of study'.]

The introduction to the 'Key Stage 3, Framework for teaching mathematics' expresses the expectation that 'teachers and trainee teachers will use it for day-to-day reference'.[3] It is permitted for teachers to depart from the framework but only where they are able to justify doing so, for, as the document points out, 'there is, after all, no point in teachers reinventing solutions to problems and challenges that are common to all'.[4] A carefully worded section[5] makes it plain that any substantial departure from the document would require a decision to be taken and defended at the departmental level, with the support of the 'school's senior managers', and so falls outside the discretion of the individual teacher.

## *Learning by fractions*

The learning model which informs the NCM is that of the individual student's (or pupil's) expanding and deepening understanding of mathematical concepts, techniques and notations, and their increasing confidence and skill in applying these techniques to problems. It seems that key ideas are introduced as early as the drafters of the NCM judge to be possible and then returned to and taken further at each Key Stage, and (if one follows the guidance provided by the Framework) during each year of the student's education, up to the end of Key Stage 3.

My observation of other teachers, and my own experience of teaching, did not persuade me that this learning model worked well and I shall use the case of fractions to illustrate how the NCM has an effect on the teaching of mathematics which is entirely contrary to the intentions of those who drafted the document. For while the aim of the learning model is to secure understanding by returning to a topic again and again in successive years, its effect is to so limit the time that can be devoted to the topic in any particular year that few students are likely to achieve an understanding of key ideas.

I was teaching, and being trained to teach, mathematics in a quite good comprehensive senior school which had a relatively strong mathematics department. The school received students in Year 9, principally from four local middle schools, and, having a large intake, divided the intake between two year groups, generating six mathematics sets in each year group. As a consequence, in Years 9, 10 and 11 (those preceding GCSE) there were two first sets, two second sets, and so on.

The first class I took over was a Set 3 in Year 9. The qualified teacher I was taking over from covered the relationship between mixed numbers and improper fractions, and multiplication and division by fractions. I then tried to explain the addition of fractions not having the same denominator. Most students got fewer than four out of the fifteen questions right in the straightforward class test which followed. We moved on to the next topic in the syllabus.

I had a second chance to teach fractions to a Set 3 in Year 9, and I approached the topic with much greater care and with a greater awareness of how extraordinarily difficult the students found it. I felt it went a little bit better but became convinced that, however the topic was presented (to a middle set in Year 9), insufficient time had been assigned to cover it.

When returning to a topic which has been introduced in previous years, one would expect to start with 'consolidation', or at least some attempt to discover what students are able to recall from their previous encounters with the topic. I seldom observed an experienced teacher attempting consolidation and I learnt from experience why this was the case. The teaching schedule allocated so little time to covering the topic, one had to launch straight into it. Too often there was almost nothing to consolidate and so one might as well treat the topic as though it was being taught for the first time. The principal emphasis in the NCM, and the various supporting documents, is on the importance of securing understanding rather than reducing mathematics to the application of seemingly arbitrary rules. I was working with good or quite good mathematicians, many of whom would have liked to have been permitted to teach mathematics in a better way, but the pressure on them was to provide rules for operating with fractions, rather than seeking to secure an understanding of the basis for these rules. (I grant that the NCM was not the only pressure which pushed teachers in this direction.) They were condemned to teach students many of whom had long ago abandoned any expectation that they would understand (in the sense of seeing why something is true) anything taught in a mathematics class. Too often the only residue which remained from their previous encounters with a topic was the memory of not having understood it last year, or the year before, or the year before that. In the two cases mentioned above, I was constrained by the teaching schedule to move on from the topic before sufficient progress had been achieved, and was conscious of having added another year to this sorry history of incomprehension. When I gave two revision classes on fractions to a Set 2 in Year 10, later in the year, students found the work quite difficult but comprehensible. However, even in this case I was forced, in the second lesson, to move on to 'five facts about circles', before I was confident that a secure understanding of fractions had been achieved. It is worth mentioning that I was encouraged to deal with the addition of fractions only after I had dealt with multiplication and division by fractions, although this reversed the order in which the topic is developed in the NCM, and it was always the addition of fractions that students found most difficult.

If you were teaching an individual child to understand fractions, and found that the child quickly grasped (perhaps through use of the number line) that a unit fraction is a number between 0 and 1 and seemed to have no difficulty with the addition of unit fractions having the same denominator, even when the result of doing so gave rise to an improper fraction, perhaps a number between 1 and 2, would you stop there? Would you not be tempted to build upon your success and move towards a discussion of the relationship between improper fractions and mixed numbers and then, perhaps, to multiplication by fractions? Would you be likely to say 'you have done very well and I look forward to returning to this topic in a year's time'?

If one fully grasps what fractions are, and has a good understanding of how the operations of addition, subtraction, multiplication and division apply to numbers, then one grasps that these operations must apply to fractions. If one knows how to add unit fractions with the same denominator then one knows that there must be a way of adding unit fractions which have a different denominator. One may be curious to know how this can be done and, even if one is not, one can make little real use of fractions until one has a fuller understanding of how to operate with them. The model of expanding and deepening a student's understanding by returning to a topic at a later stage in a syllabus has an application to many subjects, in particular to science (e.g. a notion such as valency will need to be returned to several times and each time approached at a deeper theoretical level) but is not so readily applied to mathematics.

The problem is aggravated by the fragmentation of the syllabus. The NCM could make more use of fractions in relation to other topics (e.g. areas, volumes and percentages) but chooses not to do so. How likely is one to remember something from one year to the next, if one has made no use of that knowledge in the meantime? This brings me to my second major criticism of the NCM.

## *Trying to do too much*

The syllabus is overloaded (the attainment targets too numerous) and seeks to cover too many disparate elements. Had the syllabus a narrower focus, with topics more closely interconnected, more students would end up learning and understanding more mathematics. Neither of these points is easy to argue briefly, and without close reference to the document, but the nature and extent of the vocabulary students are expected to master are, I think, indicative.

The 'Key Stage 3, Framework for teaching mathematics' concludes with vocabulary checklists. That for Year 7 (which recapitulates words used in earlier years) contains over 250 items. Under the heading 'Shape, space and measure' we have eight kinds of quadrilateral listed, including 'rhombus', 'trapezium', 'arrowhead' and 'kite'. We have 'order of rotation symmetry' under the heading 'Transformations' and under 'Handling data' not just 'range', 'mean', 'median' and 'mode', but 'frequency chart', 'modal class' and 'pie chart'. Over a hundred new words are introduced in each of Years 8 and 9. New key words introduced in Year 8 include 'associative', 'distributive', 'isometric', 'tessellate' and 'interrogate', and in Year 9 we have the introduction of terms relating to indices, simultaneous, quadratic and cubic equations, the geometry of the circle, trigonometry and, under the heading 'Handling data', 'bias', 'cumulative frequency' and 'interquartile range'.

Of course, some of the words included in these checklists are not essentially mathematical, but even if one restricts one's attention to words which have a particular meaning in a mathematical context, the size of the vocabulary children are expected to come to terms with is disconcerting and sometimes displays a whimsicality which might be charming in a less serious context. My son, at present in Year 7 and attending a local middle school, floored me with 'heptagon', which he needed to know the meaning of to do his homework. He was convinced that a heptagon was a seven-sided polygon and I was almost sure that it was not. Of course, I felt silly shortly afterwards for I should have remembered heptanes from A-Level chemistry. But since there are so few other words in common use which help one to remember this particular Greek root ('heptarchy'? 'heptasyllabic'?) and so few architects have been motivated to construct heptagonal rooms, I felt there was some excuse for my forgetfulness. I also wondered why it had been decided that every child in the country should know the meaning of this word; and should know the meaning of this word two years ahead of the time when they might find themselves in a middle set not understanding how to add fractions.

When one starts looking at the content, one finds that the oddities of the NCM go beyond whimsy. For example, there are two strands running through Ma 3 (Shape, space and measures) one of which starts from symmetries, rotations and translations and then stops, while the other starts from the geometry of the triangle (and parallelogram) and culminates in the 'five facts about circles' mentioned earlier.

The first strand starts from Ma3.3b, at Key Stage 1, which requires pupils be taught to:

> recognise movements in a straight line (translations) and rotations, and combine them in simple ways [for example, give instructions to get to the headteacher's office or for rotating a programmable toy].[6]

This strand could provide a preparation for a well known route into group theory. Is that why it's there? Who knows? Certainly not the children who are required do exercises of this sort, nor, I suspect, the staff who teach them.

The second strand (also starting at Key Stage 1) looks like a gesture towards the kind of Euclidean geometry which has been seen as an essential element in any liberal education for hundreds of years, but which is now viewed by mathematicians as suspect. Does its presence in the NCM record a partial victory of traditionalists, or educationalists, over more scrupulous pure mathematicians? Was it traditionalists who insisted that all children should learn the words 'trapezium' and 'rhombus', because they remembered learning these words at school and had happy memories of proving things in geometry? I am afraid that today's students are unlikely to have similar memories for, while the NCM requires that the relevant theorems should be proved, it does not suggest that students should be encouraged to prove things for themselves, and the only thing which is assessed is the student's capacity to use 'facts about circles' to discover a particular angle, measured in degrees, from other angles, in a complex figure. A standard text book for SEG GCSE Higher Tier Mathematics does not even mention that what it terms 'circle properties' are demonstrable.

### The need for coherence

One function that an NCM must fulfil is to provide those with a talent for mathematics with an experience of the subject which enables that talent to be recognised, and which motivates them to carry their study further. I am less worried about those students who find themselves in a first set, in a reasonably good comprehensive, for I think that, despite the NCM, they are quite likely to have an appropriate experience of the subject. A good teacher should find it possible to meet the attainment targets set by the NCM and have space to engage in various sorts of investigatory work, pursuing issues beyond the requirements of the syllabus. However, I see no prospect of this happening in middle sets and it worries me that potentially good mathematicians are probably being lost to the subject in large numbers. Without good teaching, they will even be lost from first sets. There is a danger that good students will choose other A-level subjects and students who are persuaded to continue to an A-level in mathematics (perhaps for want of a better alternative) are ill prepared for the demands of A-level work in the subject.

Another function that an NCM must fulfil is that of providing as many students as possible with some insight into the unique status of mathematics and the extraordinary role it has played in making the modern world possible. Mathematics is not, and should not be experienced as being, a range of techniques resting upon the application of arbitrary rules, for it is the one subject in the curriculum where, in principle, nothing need be accepted as true upon the authority of the teacher, or of anyone else. Overloading a syllabus, and so fully removing discretion from teachers, is unhelpful, if the aim is to achieve some understanding of what mathematics is.

How far an NCM should be constructed to meet the perceived needs of employers, I am uncertain. The large amount of time devoted to understanding different ways of presenting data in Ma 4 (pie charts etc.) is something I regret for it makes no contribution to the student's mathematical understanding. Employers want employees who are numerate (in the sense of being able to recall what the NCM calls 'number facts') and, since one can make no progress in mathematics without this capacity, in this respect their interests do not conflict with those of maths teachers. Beyond this, I think that what employers really need (as does society) are individuals who are well educated. How educative mathematics is depends less on what is taught than on how it is taught. A syllabus that is overloaded is difficult to teach well.

However one chooses to construct a syllabus for Key Stages 1 to 4, it should constitute a coherent narrative, rather than a miscellany of stories, too many of which begin 'Once upon a time ...' and then simply stop, or lamely conclude '... the King died'. Children (and students) often complain that they cannot see the point of what they are studying. It is unfortunate if their teachers cannot see the point of what they are teaching.

# What Is Science Education For?*

# David Perks

## Science education in crisis

Many agree that something needs to be done to salvage science education in the UK. A recent study by Professor Alan Smithers and Dr Pamela Robinson revealed that the number of pupils studying A-level physics has fallen by 35 per cent since 1990.[1] According to their study the trend is even more dramatic in state schools. Within higher education (HE), the furore over the loss of university science departments reached a crescendo in March 2006, when Sussex University threatened its chemistry department with closure. As Peter Atkins, professor of chemistry at Oxford University, wrote in the *Times Higher Educational Supplement*:

> How can a vice-chancellor worth his salt take one of the UK's great chemistry departments and stamp it out like an academic cockroach? How many Nobel prize-winners would it need to have before it is seen to be worth hanging on to? Why kill a department that has one of the highest research ratings in the country?[2]

Chemistry at Sussex was eventually given a reprieve after its head of department, Dr Gerry Lawless, fought a hard battle, resulting in a merger with biochemistry. But still the plight of the sciences seems dire, to the point where John Cridland, deputy director of the Confederation of British Industry (CBI), recently claimed: 'We are beginning to see UK companies saying it makes economic sense to source science graduates internationally, particularly from China

---

\*   First published in Gilland, Tony (ed.), *What is Science Education For?*, Institute of Ideas, 2006. Reprinted with some updates and additions.

and India.'[3] The CBI's director general, Richard Lambert, has identified the lack of specialist physics and chemistry teachers—only one in five science teachers has a specialist physics qualification, and one in four chemistry teachers has a specialist chemistry qualification—as a key cause for concern. Lambert warned that the government 'must set itself more challenging targets', and argued: 'we need more specialised teachers to share their enthusiasm for science and fire the imaginations of pupils, and to persuade them to study the core individual disciplines to high levels'.[4]

Science minister Lord Sainsbury, speaking to the Royal Society during Science Week in March 2006, attempted to put a gloss on the situation by pointing out that the number of graduates in computer science, medicine and biological science were all up over the last decade. However, he had to concede that the number of engineering and technology graduates had fallen by ten per cent, and graduates in physical sciences by 11 per cent, in the same decade.[5]

The UK government published its *Science and Innovation Framework 2004-2014: next steps*[6] document as part of the Budget in March 2006. The report acknowledges the worrying situation with regard to the uptake of A-level physics and chemistry, and warns: 'Declining science A-level entries have repercussions on the numbers studying science at HE. For example, those graduating with an undergraduate degree in chemistry fell by 27 per cent between 1994/95 and 2001/02, and by a further seven per cent between 2002/03 and 2004/05.'

Certainly, the government's desire to encourage more young people to go on to study the physical sciences at school and university is welcome; and the report makes a number of interesting suggestions as to how this situation can be improved. For example, the government makes a commitment to secure more physics and chemistry teachers through a drive to 'recruit science graduates into teaching via Employment Based Routes with new incentives to providers of £1,000 per recruit'. It also specifies ambitious goals for the number of pupils going on to study physics, chemistry and mathematics at A-level by the year 2014. One of the more interesting suggestions put forward is that by 2008 there should be an entitlement to study separate sciences at GCSE if a pupil achieves level 6 by the end of Key Stage 3. (Students are assessed at age 14 on a scale of 1 to 8, and the majority achieve level 5 or 6.)

However, given the drastic shortage of specialist science teachers, the fact that only about one in eight science teacher trainees is a physics graduate,[7] and the declining number of students taking the physical sciences at degree level, fulfilling these commitments is a major undertaking. For example, the government has already indicated that provision of an entitlement to study three separate sciences at GCSE will require 'collaborative arrangements with other schools, FE colleges and universities',[8] suggesting that many students will have to travel to other institutions to receive a thorough science education.

This is the context for the fact that a major reform of GCSE science education, which enforces the compulsory study of 'scientific literacy', was introduced in September 2006. All state school pupils at Key Stage 4 (aged 14-16) must be taught ideas about how science works in general—such as the nature of scientific evidence, the limitations of scientific evidence and the social and ethical issues raised by science—alongside a broad appreciation of 'organisms and health, chemical and material behaviour, energy, electricity and radiations, and the environment, Earth and universe'.[9] A range of new GCSE courses that meet these statutory requirements has been produced by the major exam boards in preparation for September 2006, and other qualifications such as BTEC diplomas have also been accredited.

The new science GCSEs have already attracted negative media coverage, with stories of independent schools abandoning them for the more traditional, subject-based international GCSEs; and much criticism has been directed at two exam boards, Edexcel and AQA, for making their examination questions solely multiple choice.[10] However, what is most striking about the reform is the justification given for it. The reason given for the change is a desire to empower students as future citizens and consumers of science, rather than to train them as future scientists—the *producers* of science. On the face of it, this motivation appears to be at odds with the desire to ensure a major increase in the number of students taking physics and chemistry at A-level and degree level. As Ken Boston, chief executive of the Qualifications and Curriculum Authority (QCA), the public body responsible for the national curriculum, argued when announcing the curriculum change: 'Previous Key Stage 4 curricula were criticised for concentrating too much on the needs of future scientists at the expense of science that is relevant to students' everyday lives.'[11]

My argument is that we have arrived at a confused and contradictory situation that threatens to undermine our ability to deliver what so many people say we need: many more students studying science to a higher level. This situation has not come out of the blue, but is the product of trends that have been developing for some time. These include:

- 'Student-centred' educational approaches leading to constant attempts to make study more 'relevant' to students' immediate lives;

- An underestimation of the capabilities of students and a desire to protect them  from failure, leading to the breaking down of subjects into 'bite-sized' chunks of digestible information at the expense of a deeper appreciation of the subjects as a whole;

- The decline of practical work and laboratory experiments;
- A disregard for the integrity of subject knowledge and an associated attempt to sideline teachers as 'knowledge intermediaries';
- Misplaced and exaggerated expectations about the role education can play in relation to wider social concerns;
- Confusion about what science has to offer society.

The impact of these broad trends on science education in schools is the focus of this essay.

## Science for citizenship?

The critical question posed at the centre of recent educational reforms is: should science education be aimed at the citizen or at the future scientist? The authors of the seminal report *Beyond 2000*, which paved the way for the introduction of the new compulsory science GCSE, were clear about their view that the training of future scientists has weighed too heavily on the teaching of science in the past:

> This report is the product of a desire to provide a new vision of an education in science for our young people. It is driven by a sense of a growing disparity between the science education provided in our schools and the needs and interests of the young people who will be our future citizens... Our view is that the form of science education we currently offer to young people is outmoded, and fundamentally is still a preparatory education for our future scientists... the ever-growing importance of scientific issues in our daily lives demands a populace who have sufficient knowledge and understanding to follow science and scientific debates with interest, and to engage with the issues science and technology poses—both for them individually, and for our society as a whole.[12]

Many of those who are concerned about the training of future scientists, including the government, are equally concerned about the engagement of the populace with science and the issues it generates. As prime minister Tony Blair said in his speech to the Royal Society in 2002: 'science is vital to our country's continued future prosperity'.[13] Blair's speech recognised not only the threat posed to the UK's position in the world by the declining number of graduates in the physical sciences, but also the threat posed by the erosion of trust in science and government. This was at the time brought sharply into focus by public hostility to genetically modified (GM) crops, summed up in Blair's assertion that people outside Britain think we are 'completely overrun by protestors and pressure groups who use emotion to drive out reason'.[14]

Given the broader uncertainty over how to handle public concerns about different aspects of science, from the MMR vaccination to animal experiments to nuclear power, it is not surprising that many are attracted by the idea of using education to solve the problem. But will it work? And what does politicising science education, through an increasing focus on issues and controversies, mean for the content of the education that students receive?

For those at the forefront of science education reform, public distrust of science seems to provide an opportunity as well as a problem. It is, they argue, by situating science education within the context of controversial debates that young people can make sense of science. As the authors of the Teaching and Learning Research Programme (TLRP) commentary *Science education in schools* claim: 'Research suggests that context-led courses lead to greater student interest, a greater appreciation of the relevance of learning to everyday life, and no measurable decrease in student understanding of science content.'[15]

The 'context-led' approach is driven by the presumed need to make science education relevant to the ordinary citizen, rather than the potential future scientist. As the report argues: 'We believe the best way forward is to provide the highest grade of "science education for citizenship" for all students.'[16] The authors go on to assert that young people who do well on such a course 'will be increasingly motivated to follow science-related careers'. Despite this upbeat assessment of the 'context-led' approach, however, the authors concede that: 'The evidence that this approach results in an increased uptake of more advanced courses is less strong.'[17]

So what evidence is there that promoting 'science education for citizenship' to a central place in the curriculum will fulfil the twin goals of engaging the interests of students in science and producing more science graduates?

A pilot study, Twenty First Century Science, was set up at 75 schools from September 2003, run by a consortium including the examining board OCR (Oxford, Cambridge and RSA Examinations), York University Education Group and the Nuffield Curriculum Centre.

In February 2005 the QCA published the results of an initial and general evaluation of the Twenty First Century Science courses that it had undertaken.[18] This evaluation consisted of one consultant visiting seven of the 75 participating pilot centres during the first year of teaching the courses, and analysis of a postal evaluation questionnaire completed by teachers at 40 of the centres at the end of the first year of teaching.

This provisional evaluation provided weak evidence that the Twenty First Century Science courses will lead to an increased uptake in students studying science beyond GCSE. The questionnaire evaluation found 'a significant minority of respondents (12 centres; 30 per cent) reported that **no more** students than usual had indicated they would take science subjects beyond GCSE' (*emphasis in original*); 20 per cent reported '**some more**' or a '**few more**' students 'had confirmed an intention to progress to post-16 science studies', and 7.5 per cent stated that 'the pilot courses had resulted in there being **fewer** than normal students wishing to progress on to post-16 studies'. The remainder were unable to answer the question for one reason or another.

However, on the other key question of concern—engagement—the evaluation found that schools and students were generally positive about the courses with 'a significant majority (33 out of the 40 centres; 82.5 per cent) of the pilot centres' reporting that they 'would recommend the pilot science GCSEs to other teachers/centres'. One primary reason given for this was that the course content was 'more relevant and up-to-date and avoids primarily targeting the needs and interests of students intending to progress on to AS/A-level science courses'. The major criticism of the courses from teachers and students was the lack of practical activity.

Given the inherent limitations of a brief evaluation of the first year of the pilot courses, it is surprising that the QCA chose not to wait for the results of the three independent reviews of Twenty First Century Science that had been commissioned before turning major elements of the pilot courses into a new programme of study shaping the future content of *compulsory* science GCSEs from September 2006.

Since then, the results of the three reviews have been published and, although broadly sympathetic to the pilot, they do not represent a ringing endorsement for the new GCSE.[19] The report raised three disturbing details about the outcome of the pilot. Firstly, fewer students agreed with the statement: '*I would trust something a scientist said* (statement B05)' after studying the new course compared with those who had not studied it. Secondly, more students agreed with the statement: '*The things we do in science make me more interested in science* (statement A04)' before they started the new course than after they had finished it. The same was true about the following statement: '*When I have a choice after GCSE, I will choose at least one science subject* (statement A05)'.

This last statement raises the prospect that the new GCSE is actually putting pupils off science rather than encouraging them to take science up at A-level and beyond. This makes the decision of the QCA to rush into adopting what the authors of the Twenty First Century Science course openly admitted was an experimental approach to science teaching quite extraordinary.

It is no surprise to me that the research raises questions about the effectiveness of the new GCSE in encouraging the uptake of science at A-level. The results of the research can only be provisional but they raise awkward questions that the proponents of the new GCSE need to answer.

I debated Professor Michael Reiss, Director of Education at the Royal Society, and a prominent supporter of the new GCSE at the Battle of Ideas conference in October 2006. He put it to me that the only way to tell if the new approach to science teaching would work was to wait and see if the numbers of students going into science at A-level started to recover. The signs are not looking good. Instead of waiting to see what happens, the advocates of academic science education need to act now if we are to stem the tide of an ill-considered reform. The alternative is too watch the incremental erosion of science education in the UK continue beyond GCSE into A-level and higher education.

## Making science 'relevant'

So why rush through such a radical change to the science curriculum, especially when we have little evidence that such a major change in direction will influence the key problem of the declining uptake of the physical sciences in schools and universities?

This shift towards promoting 'scientific literacy' over science itself is the result of deeper trends in the reform of science education, and education as a whole, which have already led to conflicting demands being placed upon the science curriculum, assessment procedures and science teachers.

One of the major demands made of education in recent years has been to make school subjects more 'relevant' to pupils. School children, it is argued, cannot be expected to engage with concepts and ideas beyond their immediate frame of reference: educationalists, therefore, should relate the subjects they teach directly to the language and ideas with which pupils are familiar in their everyday lives. It is not just educationalists who have adopted this patronising approach towards young people. The Church of England, for example, in 2005 announced plans to hold services everywhere from skateboarding parks to pubs and cafes. Not to be outdone, the Duke of Edinburgh's Award came up with slogans such as 'NE14 Fun?', 'Wanna Feel Gr8?' and 'Bored? U Wont B' in an attempt to speak to young people with 'a different voice'.[20]

The demands of 'relevance' have attracted some criticism in other disciplines. As the columnist Martin Samuel argued in *The Times* about a revision guide on Shakespeare that attempted to translate the Bard's words into teenage street-speak:

> Instead of attempting to engage the class in the work of a genius who brought such richness to our language, the entry level for the modern student is now crass and unsophisticated. Instead of trying to shake future generations out of complacency, their ignorance and lack of interest is presumed. We no longer aspire to education but to maintenance. We babysit, really, until *X Factor* begins. We depict Shakespeare as boring and obscure, then wonder why teenagers produce exam papers full of gibberish and misunderstanding.[21]

But it would seem the same disease of 'dumbing down' in the name of relevance has afflicted science education without attracting such concerns. The House of Commons Science and Technology Select Committee report, *Science Education from 14 to 19*, published in 2002, decried the double science GCSE which most students now study from 14 to 16, where all three sciences are studied together and awarded two equal GCSE grades. There are many valid criticisms to be made of double science. However, the Commons Select Committee's concern was primarily with its over-emphasis on scientific facts rather than cultural relevance:

> The GCSE science curriculum is over-prescriptive. This puts students off science because they do not have the flexibility to explore areas which interest them. It kills the interest in science which may have been kindled at primary school.[22]

Sir Gareth Roberts was commissioned by the government in 2001 to review the supply of science and engineering skills. His influential report, known as the Roberts Review, recommended that the curriculum should be reformed with the aim of 'improving the relevance of the science curriculum to pupils in order to capture the interests of pupils (especially girls) and to better enthuse and equip them to study science (particularly the physical sciences) at higher level'.[23]

Much has been made of a widely-quoted survey of A-level science students carried out by the Science Museum in 2002.[24] According to the survey, over half of students who studied double science GCSE felt it failed to make them 'curious about the world'. The survey found that most young people wanted more relevant and contemporary science, especially controversial issues. Nearly half of the respondents claimed that discussion and debate in class were the most useful ways of learning science.

What surprises me is not the fact that students complain about learning science—it was ever thus—but that today we take them seriously. Children are prone to dislike being told to do anything that demands effort from them, as any teacher or parent will confirm. It is only after they have gained something from the experience that they are going to feel any gratitude for the effort adults put into helping them achieve it.

However, something different happens if we, as educators, take pupils' complaints about science lessons on board. This brings into question the whole enterprise of trying to educate young people about science. If the children get wind of our defensiveness then they will question the purpose and value of science education still more.

There is a long tradition of educational research looking at why pupils find science hard to learn.[25] Cultural explanations for this phenomenon centre on a failure to connect with the student during the science lesson.[26] The authors of the TLRP commentary *Science Education in Schools* explain it like this:

> There can be substantial discontinuities between what young people experience in their school science lessons and in the rest of their lives.[27]

The authors go on to argue: 'Unless school science explicitly engages with the enthusiasms and concerns of... students, it will lose their interest.'

This outlook leads to the call to listen to the 'student's voice' within the classroom. As the report puts it, 'science education can only succeed when students believe that the science they are being taught is of personal worth to themselves'. But this sounds like a call to ask the students what they would like to do in their science lessons. Do we really want to hand over control of the curriculum to teenagers?

The focusing of the curriculum on controversial aspects of the implementation of science and technology, such as genetic modification or nuclear power, can no doubt provide young people with opportunity to express themselves about issues we all face. But in the absence of a thorough grasp of science and a clear understanding of its importance in the context of a particular debate, any discussion will quickly boil down to rhetorical posturing or simply confusion. Asking teenagers to make up their minds about anything is pretty daunting. But if you try to ask them to decide if we need to replace the UK's nuclear power stations, you are far more likely to get the question: 'Sir, what is nuclear power?'

There is a paradox at the heart of the debate about making science more relevant to young people. Science is widely regarded as fascinating outside of school science lessons. The sales of popular science books like Bill Bryson's *A Short History of Nearly Everything,* and the audience for TV programmes like Sky's *Brainiac Science Abuse* indicate that science is of great interest to young people. Young people have a profound interest in what science can tell them about themselves and the world around them. Whether it is the nature of evolution and the relationship between science and religion or our understanding of the history of the universe, every child is fascinated by their relationship to science.

But we don't need to flatter young people by asking them what they think about these issues. We do need to help them learn as much as they can about science, so that they can understand what science tells them about the natural world and their place in it. Where we have failed is in not translating this thirst for knowledge into more students choosing a serious academic study of the sciences, which would ultimately help all of us to come closer to answering some of these questions.

### Is science too hard?

School science can be so boring it puts young people off science for life. [28]

This was how Dr Ian Gibson, then Chairman of the House of Commons Science and Technology Committee, explained the failure to attract more young people towards science in 2002. Gibson continued: 'GCSE science students have to cram in so many facts that they have no time to explore interesting ideas.' Robin Millar and Jonathan Osborne make the same point in *Beyond 2000*, claiming that the curriculum presents science as 'a succession of "facts" to be learnt, with insufficient indication of any overarching coherence and a lack of contextual relevance to the future needs of young people'.[29]

Nobody has ever claimed that science is an easy discipline to master. But in the contemporary period science education is portrayed from all quarters as the rote learning of disconnected dry facts—so much so that even the QCA celebrates the emphasis on 'reduced content and factual recall'[30] in its new programme of study for Key Stage 4. This is leading to a fundamental redefinition of what science education is.

Millar argues that 'what citizens require is a broad, qualitative grasp of the major science explanations; the detail which many students find off-putting is rarely needed'.[31] The Twenty First Century Science pilot focuses instead on a cultural appreciation of the important stories or 'science explanations'.

According to Millar, selecting which 'science explanations' to include in the curriculum is a matter of looking at what a scientifically literate citizen ought to know about science. For Millar, the choice of which 'science explanations' to include must take seriously 'the kind of science that people encounter through the news media'. Unsurprisingly, health and medicine figure more prominently under these criteria than elementary physics or chemistry. It seems rather odd that, in putting the case for a new curriculum, Millar is prepared to argue that the mass media should have a more decisive influence on the nature of the science curriculum than the intellectual integrity of the subject.

But the key problem with this approach is its assumption that 'traditional' science teaching is just a process of asking pupils to copy and memorise facts. This belittles the effort that goes into teaching pupils to grasp what amounts to a highly abstract and difficult way of thinking about nature. Learning the sciences presents considerable challenges to young people. The role of the teacher in this is continually to challenge preconceived notions, and present new ways of thinking about the subject.

Mastery on the part of the pupil involves acquiring factual knowledge and building models to incorporate this knowledge. As children progress they begin to realise that the models they have been taught are insufficient and need to be replaced, to accommodate the new facts they are meeting about the way nature behaves. As well as refining the models they use to describe nature, students gradually become conscious of what it means to build and try out new models themselves. All the time they need to be confronted with the need to test their ideas against experimental evidence. Facilitating this process over a period of time is not the same as getting students to rote-learn dry facts. It is a question of constructing the capacity for abstract thought.

The accepted critique of 'traditional' science teaching is a shallow pastiche of the truth, and only serves to flatter the new thinking about science education. Science teaching is much more than either passing on the rote-learning of disembodied theory or the stories about science that are now being prescribed. It is about treating students as potential future scientists and providing them with the foundations of a scientific understanding of the world that will stand them in good stead whether they pursue science further or not.

## Bite-sized chunks

The extent to which educationalists have become despondent about the possibility and worth of attempting to provide students with such an opportunity to master the sciences is well reflected by the modularisation of courses and associated assessment methods.

The introduction of modular A-levels in 2000 was a major shift in the method of assessment of the sciences in schools. The split between AS and A2 examinations in the first and second year of A-levels, which went alongside modularisation, hid a further change: the lowering of the standard expected during the first year of the course to a point between GCSE and A-level. Add to this the possibility of retaking modules within the A-level course repeatedly over its duration, and the credibility of the final grades achieved is inevitably reduced.

As reported in *The Sunday Times* in December 2005, a large number of independent schools have been seriously considering abandoning the state A-level system in favour of a tougher qualification. Ralph Townsend, head of Winchester, said: 'We are concerned about the reduction in academic rigour at A-level. We want to move away from courses designed in bite-sized chunks that lack cohesion.'[32]

The triple award, or separate science examinations, offered by all the examining boards until the summer of 2006, still offered a terminal examination. However, alongside the introduction of the new programme of study for science, the QCA has seen fit to enforce the modularisation of *all* science GCSE examinations—including the separate science GCSEs. All the same arguments about fragmenting the courses and over-examining pupils are now set to resurface in the one part of the school system that had avoided these problems. In addition, there is to be a greater emphasis on coursework, which is set to rise from 20 per cent to 33 per cent under the new specifications—meaning that pupils will necessarily experience a greater assessment burden.

As made clear by the Roberts Review in 2002, students find it hard to make the progression from GCSE to A-level in the physical sciences because of the increased demands placed on the students. The changes being brought in at GCSE are likely to compromise still further the chances of students succeeding, by diluting the rigour of assessment procedures.

Sitting a single examination at the end of a two-year course may seem like a daunting prospect for a teenager, but it can provide the pressure and focus to make learning a subject meaningful. Pupils who currently sit modules in GCSE double science often have little or no idea of the examination process and find it hard to compartmentalise knowledge for each separate modular examination. With pupils sitting strings of modules at different times during the year, with little idea of how they contribute to their actual qualifications, the whole process becomes an administrative nightmare. A single terminal examination, by contrast, asks pupils to raise their game at a well-defined and pivotal moment in their school career. This pressure forces both the pupils and their teachers to consolidate their understanding of the subject, and gives pupils a chance to get to grips with the intellectual integrity of the subject as a whole. The chances of this happening with a modular scheme of assessment are heavily reduced.

Teaching separate sciences has much to offer both teachers and pupils, because it promotes subject specialists who love their discipline and can transmit their passion and knowledge through to their pupils. I have previously argued that if parents want to know how to spot a good state school, they should simply ask whether the school teaches separate science subjects.[33]

In this context we should surely be concerned about the growing gulf between the education on offer within the independent sector compared to that in many state schools.

As Boris Johnson has argued in the *Observer*: 'We are staring at a growing social iniquity that some testing academic subjects are being ghettoised in the independent sector and grammar schools.'[34] This bleak statement echoes the conclusion drawn by Professor Alan Smithers and Dr Pamela Robinson about the possible demise of physics as a subject within the state sector.[35]

It was reported in August 2005 that 15 independent schools were planning to reject the new science GCSE. According to Dr Martin Stephen, High Master of St Paul's School in London, this was on the basis that it had 'a terrifying absence of proper science'.[36] It should be of real concern to us if the independent sector thinks the new GCSEs will undermine the chances of its pupils taking science seriously.

The creation of a kind of educational apartheid is likely to be further accelerated by the adoption of the new science GCSEs. If science education is to prosper post-16, schools are going to be forced to make hard choices. Do they give students the demanding option of three separate sciences, or do they opt for the more 'relevant' suite of Twenty First Century Science courses? Under pressure to meet GCSE grade targets in order to justify specialist school status, even good schools in the state sector will think twice before offering the separate sciences.

The new science GCSEs, with their emphasis on 'scientific literacy', can only result in a negative downward pressure on the uptake of the physical sciences at both A-level and undergraduate level for pupils from state schools.

## *The death of the experimental method?*

'Are we about to say goodbye to the white coat and science laboratory in schools?'[37] I wrote in the *Times Educational Supplement* in 2006. We have already seen the invasion of the ubiquitous interactive whiteboard as the new stock in trade of most secondary school science teachers. There is great pressure on science teachers to turn to PowerPoint presentations or playing DVDs rather than doing experiments. If there is one thing that gives credence to the idea that science education involves learning too many dry facts, it is surely this trend. Unfortunately the emphasis on 'scientific literacy' seems to be exacerbating the situation.

This is all the more confusing when experimental work remains a very popular aspect of science lessons. The National Endowment for Science, Technology and the Arts (NESTA) conducted a recent study on how the manner in which children are taught science affects their learning. A major conclusion drawn from the study backs up the point that too much science is being taught as just facts on a board, rather than '... a glorious exploration of the unknown through practical experimentation'. As the authors go on to say: 'lessons are now too much based around books and not enough around bunsen burners'.[38]

Even the Science Museum survey previously discussed gave a huge thumbs-up to practical work, with 79 per cent of science students claiming it helped them to understand their science. So it would seem logical to think that the new approach to science teaching should take account of the need to reinstate the importance of practical work in science lessons. However, those at the forefront of reforming science education seem to have drawn the opposite conclusion.

Derek Bell, chief executive of the Association for Science Education and a prominent supporter of the new science GCSE, said when giving evidence to the 2002 Commons Select Committee report on *Science education from 14 to 19*: 'There is a great danger of being conned into [thinking that] the answer to it all is doing more practical work. Doing practical work in itself is not going to help children learn more effectively or motivate them.'[39] But why should the proponents of educational reforms turn away from practical work? It would seem to fly in the face of the views of the students, and the experience of most teachers.

In fact, the biggest criticism the Twenty First Century Science pilot courses received from participating teachers after its first year was the lack of practical work. As one teacher put it: 'The lack of practical activities led to pupils being "turned off".'[40] Millar himself conceded: 'If "scientific literacy" courses allocate more time to discussion of issues and analysis of data and arguments, this may inevitably impact on the time available for practical activities.'[41]

However, the decline in the practical element of science teaching is no accident or oversight. Rather, the philosophy behind the new approach to science teaching is to emphasise the pupil as a consumer of science, not as a potential scientist. The skills associated with being 'scientifically literate' are far more closely related to textual analysis and data interpretation than to experimental skills.

This is not only true of the pilot study. The new QCA programme of study for science at Key Stage 4 (GCSE) makes explicit in 'How Science Works' the kind of skills that are important to a scientifically literate citizen. Under the section 'Practical and Enquiry Skills', we can see that the laboratory experiment has been displaced by 'problem-solving and enquiry skills'. Other aspects highlighted, aside from a reference to safety issues when collecting first-hand data, focus primarily on data collection and evaluation, not experimental work. There is an emphasis on using 'secondary sources, including using ICT sources and tools'. The level of complexity involved in appreciating the experimental method is far below that acknowledged previously at Key Stage 4. The best that is put forward is the vague 'plan to test a scientific idea, answer a scientific question or solve a scientific problem'. The final element of this section gives the game away, by emphasising how pupils 'evaluate methods of collection of data and consider their validity and reliability as evidence' — in other words, discussion of scientific methods and their validity is privileged over conducting experiments.

In the context of relating 'their understanding of science to their own and others' decisions about lifestyles and to scientific and technological developments in society',[42] it is hard to escape the conclusion that what is being asked of young people is to assess conflicting opinions in the media rather than carry out experiments. In fact, the coursework components offered by the GCSE examination boards veer towards writing balanced arguments about science in the news, rather than carrying out a practical investigation.

Additionally, the emphasis on dealing with science in the context of health issues means a subtle shift in the version of science that is being presented to young people. The controlled laboratory experiment — the backbone of modern scientific enquiry — is being replaced by the field study.

The controlled laboratory experiment is the approach used to reduce scientific problems down to their simplest components and discover the laws that govern the behaviour of those components. This approach is the source of science's greatest discoveries. By comparison, the field trial of a new drug is a much less certain approach to scientific enquiry. Statistical correlations within a population, even with a control group, can only indicate a likely relationship between a new drug and an expected outcome. This is a far less powerful model of experimental science than laboratory science.

The effect of sidelining the laboratory experiment within the curriculum in favour of epidemiology can only lead to a wider acceptance of the provisional character of scientific knowledge. Scientists in this description of science become just another pressure group clutching hold of empirical data to pursue their case. But the scientific method is about much more than crude empiricism. It is about the construction of a way of looking at nature that allows us to gain increasing certainty of our understanding through testing theories against experimental data.

## What are teachers for?

Those on all sides of the debate about how we improve science education can perhaps agree on this: teachers are the most vital asset in the project of educating the next generation. As the authors of *Science Education in Schools* put it:

> The teacher is the single most important source of variation in the quality of learning.[43]

But as the Roberts Review pointed out back in 2002, there are serious concerns 'where science teachers are often required to teach areas of science that they did not study at degree level (nor, in many cases at A-level)'.[44] And as Boris Johnson argued in the *Observer* in 2006, 'it cannot be right that if you study physics in a state school, you only have a 29 per cent chance of being taught by someone with a degree in that subject'.[45]

Smithers and Robinson, in their study of the decline in physics in schools, make a clear correlation between having a well-qualified physics teacher and gaining good results:

> Teachers' expertise as measured by qualification is the second most powerful predictor of pupil achievement in GCSE and A-level physics after pupil ability.[46]

As the government made clear in its document *Science and Innovation Framework 2004-2014: next steps*, any serious attempt to address the deficit in the physical sciences must consider providing an increase in well-qualified subject specialist teachers. However, this does not appear to be prominent amongst the concerns of those promoting education for 'scientific literacy'.

The concern of the educational reform lobby is not specialist subject knowledge but what is called 'pedagogical content knowledge', or PCK. This term refers to 'the best ways of teaching specific science content and concepts to particular groups of students'.[47] Unfortunately, this does not mean learning how to do exciting laboratory experiments and demonstrations. Instead, the focus of teacher training is being redirected towards learning the new content of the 'scientific literacy' curriculum and how best to communicate those ideas to students.

Ken Boston, chief executive of the QCA, makes the case that pupils need 'transferable skills to cope with changing demands'. He argues that we should teach 'the ability to argue, to develop theories... and to ask the right questions' [48] —as though such skills can be taught in the abstract, separated from the subject matter to which they relate.

Incredibly, rather than emphasising the need to revitalise subject specialist knowledge before entering the classroom, we are told that even teachers with a good science degree need to learn different skills and ideas. Science teachers will need to teach ideas like 'the nature, processes and practices of science', which have 'traditionally been implicit rather than explicit in professional development'. Realising the size of the task they have set themselves, the advocates of reform envisage inculcating this new approach amongst teachers through 'coaching by experts, with opportunities to reflect in collegial settings on changes in classroom practice'.

Such a re-education programme for science teachers is seen as central to the success of teaching for 'scientific literacy'. As the influential educationalist Jonathan Osborne puts it:

> ... this requires the teacher to see him/herself less as a transmitter of information, reliant on a closed authoritative dialogue, and more

as a facilitator of opportunities which enable discursive consideration and exploration by students of the epistemic and cognitive dimensions of science.[49]

According to this approach, teachers should become 'knowledge intermediaries' who provide opportunities for students to 'explore and reflect on the ideas involved'. This is obviously rather different from the traditional view of a science teacher. Osborne goes on to say:

> Given that the subject-culture of science teaching is dominated by a view of science as a body of given knowledge, with little scope for argumentative discourse and where plural alternatives are rarely considered, the incorporation of 'ideas-about-science' poses a substantive challenge for the teaching of science. [50]

By stressing the discursive nature of the new science education, the advocates of reform celebrate the sidelining of teachers' expertise in their subject. They locate the central educational experience within the dialogue between pupils and teachers, rather than in an engagement with the subject as a body of knowledge. Instead of teaching the patterns between elements in the periodic table, we are supposed to encourage pupils to discuss the motivations of the different parties involved in a topical health panic like that surrounding MMR.

The problem is starkly put by Smithers and Robinson in the case of physics teaching:

> Physics in schools is at risk both through redefinition and lack of teachers with expertise in the subject.[51]

The advocates of reform may call for incentives to encourage science teachers to stay in the profession; but they are at the same time trying to turn science teachers into something they were never trained to be and in which they have no specialist knowledge. Even if the subject specialist teachers we all think we need do want to teach 'scientific literacy', it is unlikely that many will have more than the vaguest idea of how to teach or understand ethics, philosophy, media studies, cultural studies and sociology to any great depth. Asking good physics and chemistry graduates to re-train to attempt such an impossible task hardly seems the best way to make use of their knowledge and talents within the teaching profession.

## Can 'scientific literacy' rebuild civil society?

Robin Millar and Jonathan Osborne made the case for a move towards teaching for 'scientific literacy' back in 1998, in their report *Beyond 2000*. They claim that 'our future society will need a larger number of individuals with a broader understanding of science both for work and to enable them to participate as citizens in a democratic society'.[52]

According to *Beyond 2000*, science education should focus on the consumer of science rather than the producer of science. Robin Millar argues that the aim of the Twenty First Century Science pilot is to create a '"critically aware" consumer'.[53] This is explicitly targeted at a perceived democratic deficit. As he puts it:

> For citizens, the need is to be able to live and act with reasonable comfort and confidence in a society that is deeply influenced and shaped by artefacts, ideas and values of science—rather than feeling excluded from a whole area of discourse, and hence marginalised.[54]

Ken Boston, chief executive of the QCA, explains his concern 'that school science is not adequately preparing young people to arrive at informed opinions about current issues such as global climate change, the threat of a world-wide flu pandemic, the risks and benefits of nuclear power or the MMR vaccination'.[55]

To put it simply: the new science curriculum is trying to make up for the fact that politicians and scientists don't seem able to get their message across in the public arena. Teaching 'scientific literacy' is clearly seen as a counter-balance to media panics about MMR and bird flu.

Anyone who follows debates in education will be familiar with politicians' claims that education can solve every social ill imaginable. The difference in this case is that the claims are being made by people within education and not from outside. But is it sensible to base the case for educational reform on the claim that teaching 'scientific literacy' will help offset political problems?

Tony Blair is acutely aware of the dilemma politicians face when dealing with the public's attitude towards science. As he said back in 2002:

> ...Britain can benefit enormously from scientific advance. But precisely because the advances are so immense, people worry.[56]

Worrying about scientific advance is nothing new. What makes our situation unique is the depth of our current propensity to see catastrophe in technological advance. There is a general defensiveness on the part of politicians when faced with decisions about the use of science and technology: look, for example, at their sensitivity to criticisms over the building of new nuclear power stations.

But teachers can no more deal with this than politicians. Expecting teachers to be able to turn children away from the concerns associated with nuclear power or growing GM crops is asking too much of education.

It does not help matters that the proponents of 'scientific literacy' view pupils as 'consumers of science' when dealing with complex ethical dilemmas. We are in danger of encouraging only a cursory engagement with the issues in order to emphasise instead the ability of pupils to make their own decisions. This is a caricature of democracy, never mind science. Instead of empowering young people as well-informed citizens, we run the risk of setting them afloat in a sea of ethical uncertainty, with no possibility of anchoring themselves to the certainties that a scientific body of knowledge can provide.

Ironically, this approach to teaching the scientific method is in danger of assuming a level of sophistication beyond most graduates, let alone 14-year-olds. Teenagers have a simple approach to education: they want to know what the answer is. Teachers supply students with the building blocks of knowledge, which act as a foundation for their understanding. If we think we can short-circuit this process, we are mistaken. We may try to teach pupils a theoretical understanding of how scientists assess the risks associated with the introduction of new vaccinations, for example, but without a foundation of knowledge and understanding of the issues their understanding will be vastly over-simplified.

In trying to answer the question of whether complementary medicine is a sensible way to treat patients, would young people be better off with a foundation in molecular chemistry or a crude version of epidemiology? If the latter, they will inevitably end up rote-learning curtailed and largely inappropriate explanations of scientific epistemology and public health policy, which will be of little use to them outside the classroom. Disembodied theory is even more useless than dry facts.

Advocates of 'scientific literacy' go too far in claiming it can help rebuild civil society, and they underestimate the demands of debating the ethical and social complexities of contemporary scientific issues. But they have also allowed for a disturbing redefinition of science to occur. There is a school of thought that sees science as an elitist paradigm. For example Dr Jerry Ravetz, author of *Scientific Knowledge and its Social Problems* and a witness to the 2002 Commons Select Committee report on *Science Education from 14 to 19*, claimed: 'science education is one of the last surviving authoritarian social-intellectual systems in Europe'.[57]

Some within the academic community base their critique of science on the idea that knowledge is socially constructed. As a result of this perspective, it runs into conflict with science taught as objective fact rather than negotiated truth. Even though this perspective is not widely accepted within the scientific community, its influence has meant that there is defensiveness about making too strong a claim for scientific knowledge for fear of being branded elitist. Instead, both supporters and critics of science emphasise scientific 'uncertainty'. One side does so for fear of being labelled too arrogant, and the other side because it does not accept scientific objectivity.

Yet, as Lord May, a former President of the Royal Society, has argued:

> At the ever expanding frontiers, different ideas and opinions contend; the terrain is bumpy. But there are huge swathes of territory behind the frontier where evidence-based understanding has been securely achieved. For example, the Laws of Thermodynamics tell us assuredly that perpetual motion machines are impossible. In astonishing defiance of intuition, we now know that mass and energy can be interchanged, according to science's most celebrated formula, $E = mc^2$.[58]

In the context of classroom discussions of broad social concerns about science that have their own particular drivers, the focus on scientific 'uncertainty' over the vast body of knowledge that has been built up over time threatens to become a key feature of what many students will take from their experience of science education.

For example, one of the missing elements in understanding the collapse of the MMR vaccination programme in parts of the UK is that people's perceptions of risk are not solely related to their knowledge of the scientific evidence. General distrust of past authority figures, such as the medical establishment, and enthusiasm for the 'natural', as evidenced by the massive growth in the market for alternative medicines, are just two factors that have played a substantial role in influencing people's outlooks on such questions. Being complex and cultural in character, neither of these dynamics can be easily extinguished by the very certain scientific evidence about the absence of a link between the MMR vaccination and autism; other factors raise doubts in many people's minds about the validity of the evidence. This being the case in the wider society, there is no reason to think that things will be different within the classroom. Discussion of unresolved social issues like the MMR debate within the context of science classes for 14-16 year olds could easily generate real confusion about what is and is not scientifically known.

In this sense, introducing a discussion about scientific 'uncertainty' in the context of discussing controversies about science can easily compound pupils' fears about the use of science. If we don't trust what government and scientists tell us outside the classroom, are we likely suddenly to believe in it all when we go through the classroom doors? It is far more likely that teachers will meet the same general distrust of science within the classroom.

I very much doubt that studying 'scientific literacy' will either encourage young people to trust science in later life, or make them want to study it further at school and university. Yet the QCA has insisted that 'scientific literacy' must be a mandatory aspect of every child's education at GCSE since September 2006. Where does this leave science education, now and in the future?

## Science education: some principles

In this essay I have tried to make clear that, whilst many individuals and organisations are rightly concerned about the declining uptake of the physical sciences beyond GCSE and the lack of teachers with specialist qualifications in these subjects, few have grasped the confusing and contradictory trends that have been shaping science education for the last twenty years. At present, many seem to take the view that the new science GCSEs should be given a chance to demonstrate what impact they might have. Meanwhile, government promises of more subject-specialist science teachers and access to the study of three separate science GCSEs for all students achieving level 6 at Key Stage 3 are laudable, but not yet very convincing.

The hope seems to be that somehow, through the current science education reforms, we will arrive at a situation where the general populace becomes less sceptical and prone to worry about issues related to science and technology, whilst at the same time more students are trained in the sciences to a high level and become inspired to pursue careers in science and science teaching. Both aims appear to me to be wishful thinking.

In summary, my argument is that the new science GCSEs will not only fail to deliver the goal of a less anxious populace, but also, since their content and approach are built on problematic trends within science education, they will hinder our ability to pass on to students a thorough grounding in the sciences and an appreciation of what science has to offer. The relevance agenda, modularisation, a reduced emphasis on practical work, and the sidelining of teachers by re-branding them as 'knowledge intermediaries', are all antithetical to the serious task of developing a deep appreciation of scientific disciplines in a greater number of students.

There is an alternative vision for science education, based on some simple but clear statements of principle:

1. Science education should be made available to all pupils in compulsory education.

2. Science should be taught as separate subjects: physics, chemistry and biology. The courses should reflect each subject as an academic discipline in its own right.

3. Pupils should be taught by specialist subject teachers where at all possible. These are the people most likely to inspire and engage those young people in their charge.

4. 'Scientific literacy' should *not* be a compulsory element of science education in schools.

5. Given the continuation of the current allocation of 20 per cent of curriculum time to science, we should aim to cover far more content in all the three sciences, and raise our ambitions of what we can achieve with pupils in the right environment, rather than creating problems around every aspect of their learning.

6. Science courses are best examined with a single terminal examination.

These principles will lead to an extension of science, which will benefit all pupils in compulsory education by giving them a deeper understanding of science. I believe the education we give our children is a gift with which we as a society endow them. As such it should reflect the aspirations we hold out for them and for society as a whole.

Instead of foreclosing our aspirations for young people and seeing them as mere consumers of science, we will do the next generation a far greater service by daring to believe that each and every one of them can, as Steven Hawkins so eloquently put it, aspire to 'know the mind of God'.

# Notes

## Introduction

1 'Schools told to close gender gaps', *BBC News*, 17 April 2007.

2 'Pupils "must learn about nappies"', *BBC News*, 28 July 2006.

3 Meikle, J., 'Compulsory history lessons on Britain's role in slavery', *Guardian*, 2 February 2007.

4 Johnson, A., 'Children must think differently', *Independent Online*, 2 February 2007.

5 Arendt, H., *Between Past and Future*, London: Faber & Faber, 1961, p. 193.

6 These problems are discussed in Furedi, F., *Where Have All the Intellectuals Gone?*, Continuum : London, 2006.

7 'Schools discipline and pupil behaviour guidelines: guidance for schools', www.teachernet.gov.uk, see Garner, R., 'Teachers told to praise the unruly as strike looms over discipline', *Independent*, 11 April 2007.

## English As A Dialect

1 Assessment and Qualifications Alliance, *AQA Anthology: GCSE English / English Literature Specification A 2005 onwards*, Oxford: Oxford University Press, 2003.

2 Seldon, A., 'Philosophy won't do – bring on the humans', *Times Educational Supplement*, 2 February 2007.

3 Wilby, P., 'Curriculum out of the ark holds little water', *Times Educational Supplement*, 19 January 2007.

4 White, J., *What Schools Are For and Why*, Keele: Philosophy of Education Society of Great Britain, 2007.

5 Qualifications and Curriculum Authority, *Programmes of Study for English at Key Stage 3*, p. 1; http://www.qca.org.uk/secondarycurriculumreview/subject/ks3/english/index.htm

6 This is a major preoccupation in the Report of the Teaching and Learning in 2020 Review Group, *2020 Vision*, Dfes, 2006, p. 8: 'relatively few aspects of the future can be predicted with accuracy

and confidence. Meeting the challenges – both those outlined here and those yet to come – will place demands on all parts of the education system.'

7   Another similarly fashionable phrase, *independent learner*, is a contradiction in terms. Whoever learns something is dependent on the teacher and the discipline. Only after learning something does one become independent in that particular area of knowledge.

8   See 'Who examines the examiners?', *The Times*, 10 December 2005. 'Confronted by a woefully dull GCSE English anthology, Francis Gilbert and his class began to muse on the identity of those who picked their set texts'; http://www.timesonline.co.uk/article/0,,923-1916526,00.html

9   This is in line with the guidelines of the Cox Report, written to inform the first official National Curriculum in English of 1989.

10  Cox, B., *Cox on Cox: An English Curriculum for the 1990s*, London: Hodder & Stoughton, 1991, p. 71.

11  'As for the truth, Scripps, which you were worrying about: truth is no more an issue in an examination than thirst at a wine-tasting or fashion at a striptease,' is Irwin's advice to his students. Bennett, A., *The History Boys*, London: Faber and Faber, 2004, p. 26.

12  Cox, *Cox on Cox*, p. 81.

13  Cox, *Cox on Cox*, p. 18.

14  Cox, *Cox on Cox*, p. 30. (My emphasis.)

15  Cox, *Cox on Cox*, p. 30.

16  Cox, *Cox on Cox*, p. 33.

17  Cox, *Cox on Cox*, p. 33.

18  For the teachers-as-dinosaurs view: 'In *English and Englishness* Brian Doyle describes a contemporary tendency of English teachers to retreat into a museum-like or "monumental" role as professional curators of a residual "national cultural heritage".' Cox, *Cox on Cox*, p. 71.

19  Qualifications and Curriculum Authority (QCA), *The Secondary Curriculum Review: Programme of Study: English Key Stage 3*, 2007,

p. 4, downloadable version http://www.qca.org.uk/secondary curriculum_review/ subject/ks3/english/index.htm (my emphasis).

20  QCA, *The Secondary Curriculum Review: Programme of Study: English Key Stage 3*, 2007, p. 4. Exactly the same note appears in the current version of the National Curriculum for England; www.nc.uk.net

21  Cox, *Cox on Cox*, p. 32.

22  Smithers, R., 'Birdwatching and cookery on personalised timetable', *Guardian*, 6 February 2007.

23  Smithers, R., 'Birdwatching and cookery on personalised timetable', *Guardian*, 6 February 2007.

24  Branigan, T., 'Shakespeare and algebra are a must for all pupils, schools told', *Guardian*, 5 February 2007.

**Geography Used To Be About Maps**

1  Bednarz, S. (2003) 'Citizenship in the Post-9/11 United States: A Role for Geography Education?', *International Research in Geographical and Environmental Education*, 12 (1), 72-80, p. 74.

2  Mitchell, K., (2003) 'Educating the National Citizen in Neoliberal Times: From the Multicultural Self to the Strategic Cosmopolitan', *Transactions of the Institute of British Geographers*, 28, 387-403; Linklater, A., 'Cosmopolitan Citizenship', in Isin, E. and Turner, B. (eds) *Handbook of Citizenship Studies*, Thousand Oaks, CA: Sage, 2002, pp. 317-32.

3  See, Standish, A., (2003) 'Constructing a Value Map', *Geography*, 88 (2), 149-152.

4  Cited in Hunter, J., *The Death of Character: Moral Education in an Age Without Good or Evil*, New York: Basic Books, 2000, p. 63.

5  Advisory Group on Citizenship, *Education for Citizenship and the Teaching of Democracy in Schools: Final Report of the Advisory Group on Citizenship*, London: Qualifications and Curriculum Authority, 1998, p. 7.

6  For instance see, Wilkinson, H. and Mulgan, J., *Freedom's Children: Work, Relationships and Politics for 18-34 Year Olds in Britain Today*, London: Demos, 1995.

7   Advisory Group on Citizenship, *Education for Citizenship and the Teaching of Democracy in Schools*, 1998, p. 10.

8   Qualifications and Curriculum Authority, *About the Citizenship Attainment Targets*, 2006. http://www.ncaction.org.uk/subjects/citizen/targets.htm

9   Isin, E. and Turner, B., *Handbook of Citizenship Studies*, Thousand Oaks, CA: Sage, 2002.

10  Qualifications and Curriculum Authority, *National Curriculum online: Citizenship, Key Stage 3*, 2006. http://www.nc.uk.net/webdav/harmonise?Page/@id=6001&Session/@id=D_WedHJXqXFlewmkBCzl85&POS[@stateId_eq_main]/@id=4165&POS[@stateId_eq_note]/@id=4165 [visited 12/7/06].

11  See, Grimwade K., Reid, A. and Thompson, L., *Geography and the New Agenda*, Sheffield: Geographical Association, 2000.

12  International Geographic Union/Commission on Geographic Education, *International Charter on Geographic Education*, Brisbane, IGU/CGE, 1992, cited in, Edwards, 'Geography, Culture, Values and Education', in Gerber, R. and Williams, M. (eds), *Geography, Culture and Education: Introduction*, London: Kluwer Academic Publications, 2002, p. 31.

13  Geographical Association (1999) 'Geography in the Curriculum: A Position Statement', *Teaching Geography*, 24(2), 57-59.

14  Westaway, J. and Rawling, E., 'A New Look for GCSE Geography', *Teaching Geography*, April 2003.

15  Oxford, Cambridge and RSA Examinations, *Specification Content: GCSE Geography (Pilot)*, Oxford, Cambridge and RSA Examinations, 2004.

16  Orr, D., *Earth In Mind: On Education, Environment, and the Human Prospect*, Washington DC: Island Press, 1994; Paden, M., 'Education for Sustainability and Environmental Education', in: Wheeler, K. and Bijur, A. (eds), *Education for a Sustainable Future: A Paradigm Of Hope for the 21st Century*, New York: Kluwer Academic/ Plenum Publishers, 2000; Smith, G. and Williams, D., *Ecological Education in Action: On Weaving Education, Culture and the Environment*, Albany, NY State: University of New York Press, 1999.

17  Sitarz, D., *Agenda 21: The Earth Summit Strategy to Save Our Planet*, Boulder, Colorado: Earthpress, 1993, pp. 294-95.

18  Oxford, Cambridge and RSA Examinations, *Specification Content: GCSE Geography (Pilot)*, Oxford, Cambridge and RSA Examinations, 2004.

19  Edexcel, Specifications for GCSE in Geography A: First Examination 2003, London: Edexcel Foundation, 2000.

20  Assessment and Qualifications Alliance, *GCSE Geography Specification A*, 2002, p. 13. http://www.aqa.org.uk/qual/pdf/AQA-3031-3036-W-SP-04.pdf [visited May 30, 2003]

21  McNaught, A. and Witherick, M., *Global Challenge: A2 Level Geography for Edexcel B*, Harlow: Longman, 2001.

22  Agnew, J. (2003) 'Contemporary Political Geography: Intellectual Heterdoxy and its Dilemmas', *Political Geography*, 22, 603-606; Painter, J. (2003) 'Towards a Post-disciplinary Political Geography', *Political Geography*, 22, 637-639.

23  Nuffield Foundation, 'Citizenship Through Geography', Nuffield Foundation, 2006.

24  Lidstone, J. and Stoltman, J. (2002) 'International Understanding and Geographical Education', *International Research in Geographical and Environmental Education*, 11(4), 309-312.

25  Stromquist, N., *Education in a Globalized World: The Connectivity of Economic Power, Technology, and Knowledge*, New York: Rowman & Littlefield, 2002.

26  Mortensen, L., 'Global Change Education: Education Resources for Sustainability', in Wheeler and Bijur (eds), *Education for a Sustainable Future*, 2000.

27  Wilbanks, T. (1994) 'Sustainable Development in Geographic Context', *Annals of the Association of American Geographers*, 84, 541-557.

28  Bednarz, S. (2003) 'Citizenship in the Post-9/11 United States: A Role for Geography Education?', *International Research in Geographical and Environmental Education*, 12 (1), 72-80, pp. 76-77.

29  Ravitch, D. and Viteritti, J., *Making Good Citizens: Education and Civil Society*, New Haven: Yale University Press, 2001.

30  Cotton, K. (1996) 'Educating for Citizenship', *School Improvement Research Series*. www.nwrel.org/scpd/sirs/10/c019.html [visited 4/1/04]; Braungart, R. and Braungart, M., 'Citizenship Education in the United States in the 1990s', in: Ichilov, O. (ed.), *Citizenship and Citizenship Education in a Changing World*, Portland, OR: Woburn, 1998.

31  Ravitch and Viteritti, *Making Good Citizens: Education and Civil Society*, 2001.

32  See, Pupavac, V., 'The Demoralised Subject of Global Civil Society', in Gideon, B. and Chandler, C. (eds), *Global Civil Society: Contested Futures*, Routledge, 2004.

33  See, Hirst, P., *Knowledge and the Curriculum*, London: Routledge and Kegan Paul, 1974.

34  Dorsey, B. (2001) 'Linking Theories of Service-Learning and Undergraduate Geography Education', *Journal of Geography*, 100, 124-132.

35  Cited in Hunter, J., *The Death of Character: Moral Education in an Age Without Good or Evil*, New York: Basic Books, 2000, p. 62.

36  Smith, D., *Moral Geographies: Ethics in a World of Difference*, Edinburgh: Edinburgh University Press, 2000.

37  See, McHoul, A. and Grace, W., *A Foucault Primer: Discourse, Power and the Subject*, New York: New York University Press, 1993.

38  See, McHoul and Grace, *A Foucault Primer: Discourse, Power and the Subject*, 1993.

39  Smith, *Moral Geographies: Ethics in a World of Difference*, 2000.

40  Philo, cited in Smith, D. (1997) 'Geography and Ethics: A Moral Turn?', *Progress in Human Geography*, 21(4), 583-590.

41  Rasmussen, C. and Brown, B., 'Radical Democractic Citizenship: Amidst Political Theory and Geography', in Isin and Turner (eds), *Handbook of Citizenship Studies*, 2002, p. 182.

42  Kirman, J. (2003) 'Transformative Geography: Ethics and Action in Elementary and Secondary Geography Education', *Journal of Geography*, 102, 93-98, p. 93.

43  Dowler, L. (2002) 'The Uncomfortable Classroom: Incorporating Feminist Pedagogy and Political Practice into World Regional Geography', *Journal of Geography*, 101, 68-72, p. 68.

44  Gerber, R. and Williams, M. (eds), *Geography, Culture and Education: Introduction*, London: Kluwer Academic Publications, 2002, p. 1.

45  Steinberg, P. (1997) 'Political Geography and the Environment', *Journal of Geography*, 96(2), 113-118, p. 118.

46  Fien, J., 'Education for Peace Through Geography', in Naish, M. (ed.), *Geography and Education: National and International Perspectives*, London: Institute of Education, 1992.

47  Lambert, D., 'Geography and the Informed Citizen', in Gerber and Williams, (eds) *Geography, Culture and Education: Introduction*, 2002, p. 97.

48  United Nations Convention on the Rights of the Child, *Convention on the Rights of the Child*, Office of the High Commissioner for Human Rights, 1989.

49  Holloway, S. and Valentine, G., *Children's Geographies: Playing, Living, Learning*, London: Routledge, 2000.

50  Catling, S. (2003) 'Curriculum Contested: Primary Geography and Social Justice', *Geography*, 88(3), 164-210.

51  Catling, 'Curriculum Contested: Primary Geography and Social Justice', p. 190.

52  Qualifications and Curriculum Authority, *National Curriculum online: Citizenship, Key Stage 3*, 2004. http://www.nc.uk.net/webdav/harmonise?Page/@id=6001&Session/@id=D_Ju8L31r6rqPiBrgkF5p6&POS[@stateId_eq_main]/@id=4165&POS[@stateId_eq_note]@id=4165 [visited 23/11/04]

53  Mitchell, K. (2003) 'Educating the National Citizen in Neoliberal Times: From the Multicultural Self to the Strategic Cosmopolitan', *Transactions of the Institute of British Geographers*, 28, 387-403, p. 387.

54  Pupavac, V., 'From Statehood to Childhood: Regeneration and Changing Approaches to International Order', in Pugh, M. (ed.), *Regeneration of War-Affected Societies*, London: Macmillan, 2000, p. 146.

55  Pupavac, 'From Statehood to Childhood: Regeneration and Changing Approaches to International Order', 2000, p. 146.

56  See, Standish, A., 'Losing the Plot – Children's Geography', *Spiked-online*, 30 March 2004. http://www.spiked-online.com/Articles/0000000CA4A8.htm

57  Advisory Group on Citizenship, *Education for Citizenship and the Teaching of Democracy in Schools: Final Report of the Advisory Group on Citizenship*, London: Qualifications and Curriculum Authority, 1998.

58  Furedi, F., *Therapy Culture: Cultivating Vulnerability in an Age of Uncertainty*, London and New York: Routledge, 2003.

59  Machon, P. and Walkington, H., 'Citizenship: The Role of Geography?', in Kent, A. (ed.), *Reflective Practice in Geography Teaching*, London: Paul Chapman Publishing, p. 184.

60  Chandler, D., *Constructing Global Civil Society: Morality and Power in International Relations*, Palgrave McMillian, 2004.

61  For instance, see, Oxfam, *A Curriculum for Global Citizenship*, Oxford: Oxford Development Education Programme, 2000.

62  Chandler, *Constructing Global Civil Society: Morality and Power in International Relations*, 2004.

63  Chandler, D., *From Kosovo to Kabul: Human Rights and International Intervention*, London: Pluto Press, 2002; Duffield, M., *Global Governance and the New Wars: The Merging of Development And Security*, New York: Zed Books, 2001.

64  Hammersley, M. (1999) 'Some Reflections on the Current State of Qualitative Research', *Research Intelligence*, 70, 16-18, p. 18.

65  Veck, W., 'What are the Proper Ends of Educational Inquiry: Research for Justice, for Truth, or Both?', paper presented to Biennial Conference of the International Network of Philosophers of education, Oslo, 9 August 2002.

66 Veck, W., 'What are the Proper Ends of Educational Inquiry: Research for Justice, for Truth, or Both?', paper presented to Biennial Conference of the International Network of Philosophers of education, Oslo, 9 August 2002.

67 Furedi, *Therapy Culture: Cultivating Vulnerability in an Age of Uncertainty*, 2003.

**The New History Boys**

1 Mary Price, 'History in Danger', *History*, Vol. LIII, p. 342.

2 Schools Council History 13-16 Project, 'A New Look at History', 1976, p. 9.

3 'A New Look at History', 1976, p. 9.

4 'A New Look at History', 1976, p. 36.

5 See for example: *Hansard* ,House of Lords, cols 1096 to 1114, 21 July 1989.

6 Available to listen to on the RSA website: www.rsa.org.uk.

7 www.bbc.co.uk/pressoffice and *Guardian*, 5 August 2004.

8 Reported in the *Sunday Telegraph*, 16 June 2003.

9 Reported in the *Daily Telegraph*, 18 January 2001.

10 *Curriculum Review: Diversity and Citizenship*, DfES, 2007.

11 From: School History Project's 'On-line resource for teachers' (www.leedstrinity.ac.uk/shp/ResourcesGCSE/index.htm).

12 Quoted in Schama, S., *Citizens*, Penguin Books, 1989, p. xiii.

13 Dearing, R., *The National Curriculum and Its Assessment: Final Report.* 1994, p. 63.

14 Dearing, *The National Curriculum and Its Assessment*, 1994, p. 67.

15 Thatcher, M., *The Downing Street Years*, Harper Collins, 1993, p. 593.

16 Thatcher, *The Downing Street Years*, 1993, p. 594.

17 Thatcher, *The Downing Street Years*, 1993, p. 595.

18 Thatcher, *The Downing Street Years*, 1993, p. 596.

19 *Secondary Curriculum Review,* February 2007. The statutory programme of study is to be published in autumn 2007 for teaching in autumn 2008.

20 *Times Educational Supplement,* 9 February 2007.

21 See Appendix 2 for a full list.

22 *Times Educational Supplement,* 26 February 1999.

23 Quoted in Gardham, D. and Paton, G., 'Schools ignoring birthday of two kingdoms', *Daily Telegraph,* 4 January 2007.

24 Quoted in *Daily Telegraph,* 4 January 2007.

25 *Times Educational Supplement,* 24 March 2000.

26 Garner, R., 'Alarm at slump in number of pupils studying history', *Independent,* 13 February 2007.

27 *Independent,* 13 February 2007.

28 McGovern, C., 'O' levels are alive and well – but not in Britain', *Daily Telegraph,* 7 June 2006.

29 Reported online BBC News/Education, 14 February 2007.

30 House of Lords *Hansard,* 27 March 2000.

31 Reported in the *Daily Telegraph,* 10 October 2006.

32 E.g. *Coursework and Teachers Guide,* Issue 4, Edexcel Board.

33 Research paper by Farrell, A. and Jesson, D., October 2006, available from afarrell.eng@st-ives.cornwall.sch.uk

## Foreign Languages Without Tears?

1 CILT/ALL Language Trends Survey 2006; http//www.cilt.org.uk/key/trends2006htm

2 Maclure, S., *Education Reformed: A Guide to the Education Reform Act,* London: Hodder and Stoughton, 1988, p.169.

3 Wicksteed, K, 'Primary languages: will it work?', *The Linguist,* Vol. 44, No. 11, 2005, pp. 2-4.

4    http://www.teachernet.gov.uk/teachingand learning/
     subjects/languages/languagesreview/

5    Williams, K., *Why Teach Foreign Languages in Schools?* Impact No.5,
     Philosophy of Education Society of Great Britain, 2000. p. 1.

6    Hawkins, E., *Modern Languages in the Curriculum,* Cambridge:
     Cambridge University Press, 1987, p. 32.

7    Lawes, S., 'The Unique Contribution of Modern Foreign Languages
     to the Curriculum', in Field, K. (ed.), I*ssues in Modern Foreign
     Languages Teaching,* London: RoutledgeFalmer, 2000.

8    Milton, J. and Meara, P., 'Are the British Really Bad at Learning
     Foreign Languages?', in *Language Learning Journal,* No. 18,
     Association for Language Learning, December 1998.

9    Graham, S., 'Experiences of learning French: a snapshot at Years 11,
     12 and 13', in *Language Learning Journal* No. 25, Summer 2002,
     Association for Language Learning.

### Teaching By Numbers

1    DfEE and QCA, *Mathematics: The National Curriculum for England,*
     Stationery Office, 1999, p. 2, quoted from the Education Act 1996,
     section 354a.

2    *NCM,* p. 6.

3    *Framework for Teaching Mathematics: Years 7, 8 and 9,* DfEE, 2001,
     p. 3.

4    *FM,* p. 2.

5    *FM,* p. 3.

6    *NCM,* p. 19.

### What Is Science Education For?

1    Smithers, A. and Robinson, P., *Physics in Schools and Universities 2:
     Patterns and Policies,* Centre for Education and Employment,
     University of Buckingham, August 2006;
     http://www.buckingham.ac.uk/education/research/ceer/pdfs/physi
     csprint-2.pdf

2   Atkins, P., 'Stop counting beans, start planting trees', *Times Higher Educational Supplement*, 17 March 2006.

3   'UK looking overseas for science graduates', *Education Guardian*, 15 March 2006.

4   'UK's World Class Science Base Under Threat as Young People Turn Their Back on Science', CBI Press Release, 14 August 2006

5   Presentation given by Lord Sainsbury, March 2006; http://www.royalsoc.ac.uk/page.asp?tip=1&id=4207

6   *Science and Innovation Framework 2004-2014: next steps*, HM Treasury, 22 March 2006; http://www.hm-treasury.gov.uk/media/D2E/4B/bud06_science_332v1.pdf

7   Smithers and Robinson, *Physics in Schools and Universities 2*, 2006.

8   *Science and Innovation Framework 2004-2014*, HM Treasury, 22 March 2006.

9   Programme of study: science, Key Stage 4, QCA, 2006; http://www.qca.org.uk/downloads/10340_science_prog_of_study_from_2006_ks4.pdf

10  For example see 'Top independent school to ditch GCSE science', Rebecca Smithers, *Guardian*, 3 September 2005; and 'Pass this GCSE without writing a word', Liz Lightfoot, *Daily Telegraph*, 10 June 2006.

11  *Science: Changes to the Curriculum from 2006 for Key Stage 4*, Foreword by Ken Boston, QCA, 2005.

12  Millar, R. and Osborne, J., *Beyond 2000*, King's College, London, 1998; http://www.kcl.ac.uk/education/publications/bey2000.pdf

13  Tony Blair, Speech to the Royal Society, 23 May 2002; http://politics.guardian.co.uk/speeches/story/0,11126,721029,00.html

14  Blair, Speech to the Royal Society, 23 May 2002.

15  *Science Education in Schools: Issues, Evidence and Proposals*, Teaching and Learning Research Programme, 2006, p. 9.

16  *Science Education in Schools*, TLRP, 2006, p. 4.

17  *Science Education in Schools*, TLRP, 2006, p. 9.

18  *Evaluation and Analysis of the Science for the 21st Century Pilot GCSEs*, QCA, February 2005.

19  *The Twenty First Century Science Pilot Evaluation Report*, UYSEG and Nuffield Foundation, February 2007; (see http://www.21stcenturyscience.org/data/files/c21-evaln-rpt-feb07-10101.pdf).

20  Claire Fox, 'Hey, Miss, this homework just ain't relevant', *The Times*, 22 October 2005.

21  'Romeo, wherefore art thou talking stupid?' *The Times*, 6 June 2006; http://www.timesonline.co.uk/newspaper/0,,2741-2212127_2,00.html

22  *Science Education from 14 to 19*, House of Commons Science and Technology Committee, Third Report of Session 2001-02, vol. I, p. 15.

23  The Roberts Review, *SET for Success*, 2002, HM Treasury, p. 6; http://www.hm-treasury.gov.uk/media/643/FB/ACF11FD.pdf

24  'Planet Science Student Review of the Curriculum', 2002; http://www.planet-science.com/sciteach/review/Findings.pdf

25  Driver, R., Leach, J., Millar, R. and Scott, P., *Young People's Images of Science*, Oxford University Press, 1996.

26  Aikenhead, G., 'Science education: border crossing into the subculture of science', in *Studies in Science Education*, vol. 27, 1996, pp. 1-52.

27  *Science Education in Schools*, TLRP, 2006, p. 5.

28  'Science lessons tedious and dull', BBC News, 11 July 2002; http://news.bbc.co.uk/1/hi/education/2120424.stm

29  Millar and Osborne, *Beyond 2000*, 1998, p. 4.

30  QCA presentation on changes in 2006; http://www.qca.org.uk/downloads/14008_presentation_changes_to_Science_June_2005.ppt

31  Millar, R., 'Twenty First Century Science: Insights from the design and implementation of a scientific literacy approach in school

science', *International Journal of Science Education*, vol. 28, issue 13, October 2006, pp. 1499-1521.

32 'Top private schools to drop 'easy' A-levels', *The Sunday Times*, 11 December 2005.

33 Perks, D., 'Let's get physical', *Spiked*, 11 September 2003; http://www.spiked-online.com/Articles/00000006DF11.htm

34 Johnson, Boris, 'A teaching scandal we can't afford', *Observer*, 9 July 2006.

35 Smithers, A. and Robinson, P., *Physics in Schools and Colleges: Teacher Deployment and Student Outcomes*, Centre for Education and Employment, University of Buckingham, November 2005, p. iv. http://www.buckingham.ac.uk/education/research/ceer/pdfs/physi csprint.pdf

36 'At least 15 schools to snub GCSE science exam', *Independent*, 6 August 2005.

37 Perks, David, 'Dark forces in the lab', *Times Educational Supplement*, 6 January 2006.

38 Kestenbaum, J., *A Mission for Innovation: Fostering Science Enquiry Learning Across the UK*, CEO of National Endowment for Science, Technology and the Arts (NESTA), 2006. http://www.nesta.org.uk/inspireme/think_jk_june06.html

39 *Science Education from 14 to 19*, House of Commons Science and Technology Committee, Third Report of Session 2001-02, vol. I, p. 20.

40 Millar, 'Twenty First Century Science: Insights from the design and implementation of a scientific literacy approach in school science', *International Journal of Science Education*, 2006.

41 Millar, 'Twenty First Century Science: Insights from the design and implementation of a scientific literacy approach in school science', *International Journal of Science Education*, 2006.

42 Programme of study: science, Key Stage 4, QCA, 2006; http://www.qca.org.uk/downloads/10340_science_prog_of_study_ from_2006_ks4.pdf

43 *Science Education in Schools*, TLRP, 2006, p. 11.

44  The Roberts Review, *SET for Success*, 2002, p. 4, paragraph 0.17. http://www.hm-treasury.gov.uk/media/643/FB/ACF11FD.pdf

45  Johnson, Boris, 'A teaching scandal we can't afford', *Observer*, 9 July 2006.

46  Smithers and Robinson, *Physics in Schools and Colleges*, 2005, Executive summary, p. i.

47  *Science Education in Schools*, TLRP, 2006, p. 12.

48  Boston, Ken, 'A catalyst for change in the school science', *Daily Telegraph*, 8 March 2006.

49  Millar, R., 'Towards Evidence-Based Practice in Science Education 3', *Teaching and Learning: Research Briefing*, no. 3, Teaching and Learning Research Programme, www.tlrp.org, June 2003.

50  *Teaching and Learning: Research Briefing*, no. 3, June 2003.

51  Smithers and Robinson, *Physics in Schools and Colleges,* 2005, p. iv.

52  Millar and Osborne, *Beyond 2000*, 1998, p. 8.

53  Millar, 'Twenty First Century Science: Insights from the design and implementation of a scientific literacy approach in school science', *International Journal of Science Education*, 2006.

54  Millar, 'Twenty First Century Science: Insights from the design and implementation of a scientific literacy approach in school science', *International Journal of Science Education,* 2006.

55  Boston, Ken, 'A catalyst for change in the school science', *Daily Telegraph*, 8 March 2006.

56  Tony Blair, Speech to the Royal Society, 23 May 2002.

57  *Science Education from 14 to 19*, House of Commons Science and Technology Committee, 3rd Report of Session 2001-02, vol. I,  p. 16.

58  'Threats to Tomorrow's World', President's Anniversary Address 2005, Lord May of Oxford, Royal Society, 30 November 2005.

# Index